Speedsolving
the Cube

Easy-to-Follow, Step-by-Step Instructions for Many Popular
3-D Puzzles

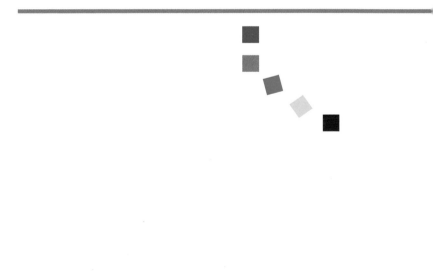

Speedsolving
the Cube

Easy-to-Follow, Step-by-Step Instructions for Many
Popular 3-D Puzzles

Dan Harris

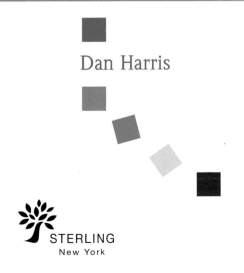

STERLING
New York

STERLING
New York

An Imprint of Sterling Publishing
387 Park Avenue South
New York, NY 10016

ISBN 978-1-4027-5313-8

Library of Congress Cataloging-in-Publication Data
Harris, Dan, 1985
Speedsolving the cube: easy-to-follow, step-by-step instructions for many poular 3-D puzzles / Dan Harris.
p. cm.
Includes index.
ISBN-13: 978-1-4027-5313-8
ISBN-10: 1-4027-5313-6

GV1507.R83H37 2008
793.74-dc22
2007032214

Distributed in Canada by Sterling Publishing
c/o Canadian Manda Group, 165 Dufferin Street
Toronto, Ontario, Canada M6K 3H6
Distributed in the United Kingdom by GMC Distribution Services
Castle Place, 166 High Street, Lewes, East Sussex, England BN7 1XU
Distributed in Australia by Capricorn Link (Australia) Pty. Ltd.
P.O. Box 704, Windsor, NSW 2756, Australia

For information about custom editions, special sales, and premium and corporate purchases, please contact Sterling Special Sales at 800-805-5489 or specialsales@sterlingpublishing.com.

Manufactured in China

20 19 18 17 16 15 14

www.sterlingpublishing.com

Dedication

This book is dedicated to
Lisa Aldridge and Ron van Bruchem.

Contents

CHAPTER 5
A Speedcubing Method for Solving
the 3×3×3 Rubik's Cube 40

CHAPTER 6
Expert 3×3×3 Speedcubing Techniques 70

CHAPTER 8
A Method to Solve Rubik's Professor Cube (5×5×5) 121

CHAPTER 9
A Method to Solve Rubik's Mini Cube (2×2×2) 138

About the Author

Dan Harris is one of the world's leading experts in the field of "speedcubing," which is the term used to describe the solving of Rubik's Cube and other related twisty-puzzles against the clock. Since taking up speedcubing in 2002, Dan quickly rose through the ranks to become one of the world's best twisty-puzzle solvers. In 2003 he participated in the second Rubik's World Championships, finishing a respectable 29th out of a field of almost 100. Since then he has taken part in 2 further world events, 2 European championships, and several national competitions hosted around the globe, culminating in his first tournament win after several near misses at the Italian Open 2007, hosted in Rome. He is the current UK record holder for several Rubik's events, including the fastest solve of a 3×3×3 Rubik's Cube at 10.59 seconds, which was also the fastest individual 3×3×3 solve of the 2007 World Championships, held in Budapest. Dan has years of experience in the methods behind the magic of Rubik's Cube, and in this book he presents a host of information designed to help you not only solve your puzzles but solve them fast!

2

A Short History of Rubik's Cube and "Speedcubing"

The time: 1974.
The place: Budapest.
The man: Ernö Rubik.

That frustrating plastic puzzle made up of 6 sides and 54 different-colored stickers came into being as the brainchild of Professor Rubik, Hungarian lecturer of architecture. Although a patent application was drafted in 1974 and applied for in 1975, it wasn't until 1977 that the "Magic Cube" was first seen on shelves in Hungarian toy shops. One of the main problems faced by Rubik was finding a manufacturer who could take on the complex task of mass-producing the puzzle with all of its inner and outer complexities. During 1978 and 1979, the Magic Cube's popularity spread like wildfire throughout Hungary, even drawing attention from the Western World, where it was stirring interest among the ranks of academics and mathematicians. Thanks to the efforts of two great men, Dr. Tibor Laczi and Tom Kremer, the Magic Cube finally made its international debut in 1980 at the toy fairs of London, New York, Paris, and Nuremberg. Between 1980 and 1982 an estimated 100 million cubes were sold worldwide. It was renamed "Rubik's Cube" and has proceeded to taunt millions of frustrated puzzlers and enchant dedicated enthusiasts across the globe for over two decades.

It was not long after the cube's international launch that several talented puzzle solvers figured out various systems and solutions to solve it and began competing against one another to see who could solve the cube in the fastest time. The sport of speedcubing was born and the first championships were held in the UK in 1981. The grand prize was a trip to the upcoming World Championships, and Julian Chilvers won with a fastest time of 25.79 seconds. In 1982 the inaugural Rubik's World Championships were held in Budapest, with competitors from 19 different nations taking part. The competition was a roaring success, and the title was taken by Vietnamese-American Minh Thai with a best time and world record of 22.95 seconds. Afterward, the cube craze began to die away, and by the 1990s it was a long-forgotten artifact forever associated with '80s culture.

Fortunately for everyone concerned, the cube was reborn in 2003, thanks to the incredible efforts of Canadian speedcuber Dan Gosbee, who organized the second Rubik's World Championships, held in Toronto, Canada. A few years earlier, some die-hard speedcubers from the 1980s, together with some up-and-coming speedcubers, joined to form an online speedcubing community, but it was the 2003 event that really launched Rubik's Cube back onto the world stage. In all, 83 participants from 15 different countries took part, competing with not only the standard $3\times3\times3$ cube but also the $4\times4\times4$, $5\times5\times5$, Rubik's Magic, and Rubik's Clock, among others. The winner of the $3\times3\times3$ event was Dan Knights, a software engineer from the United States, with an average time in the final of exactly 20.00 seconds. Dan also held the single-solve world record until it was broken by Danish puzzler Jess Bonde in an incredible 16.53 seconds at the same event. The number of competitions and competitors has dramatically increased over the past few years, riding on the success of the 2003 World Championships. Not long after, Ron van Bruchem founded the World Cube Association, which is the governing body that, along with delegates in each participating country, oversees every official Rubik's competition held around the globe.

As of 2007, over 2,000 people have competed in a Rubik's Cube championship, and in 2006 alone, 33 different competitions took place around the globe. Since its rebirth, sales have increased year upon year, and alongside them, the sport of speedcubing has grown to become more popular and active now than at any other time in the puzzle's history.

RUBIK'S CUBE (3×3×3)
SPEEDCUBING FACTS AND FIGURES

Rubik's 3×3×3 World Champions—Past and Present			
Year	World Champion	Winning Time (seconds)	All Results in Final (seconds)
1982	Minh Thai, USA	22.95*	27.16, 22.95, 27.97
2003	Dan Knights, USA	20.00	21.13, 19.93, 18.95, 22.07, 18.76
2005	Jean Pons, France	15.10	15.62, 15.87, 13.00, 13.81, 18.59
2007	Yu Nakajima, Japan	12.46	11.50, 13.43, 14.38, 12.16, 11.78

*Minh Thai's win was based on a single time; all other competitions are based on a mean of 3, after removing the fastest and the slowest times.

Rubik's 3×3×3 European Champions—Past and Present			
Year	European Champion	Winning Time (seconds)	All Results in Final (seconds)
2004	Lars Vandenbergh, Belgium	16.19	17.01, 15.63, 19.25, 15.93, 14.95
2006	Joël van Noort, Netherlands	14.97	20.78, 13.83, 14.93, 15.07, 14.91

Rubik's 3×3×3 World Record Holders—Past and Present		
Date	World Record Holder	World Record Time (seconds)
November 2007	Ron van Bruchem, Netherlands	**9.55**
October 2007	Erik Akkersdijk, Netherlands	9.77
May 2007	Thibaut Jacquinot, France	9.86
February 2007	Edouard Chambon, France	10.36
August 2006	Toby Mao, USA	10.48
January 2006	Leyan Lo, USA	11.13
October 2005	Jean Pons, France	11.75
April 2004	Shotaro Makisumi, Japan	12.11
April 2004	Shotaro Makisumi, Japan	13.93
January 2004	Shotaro Makisumi, Japan	14.76
January 2004	Shotaro Makisumi, Japan	15.07
August 2003	Jess Bonde, Denmark	16.53
August 2003	Dan Knights, USA	16.71
June 1982	Minh Thai, USA	22.95

RUBIK'S REVENGE (4×4×4)
SPEEDCUBING FACTS AND FIGURES

Rubik's 4×4×4 World Champions—Past and Present

Year	World Champion	Winning Time (minutes:seconds)	All Results in Final (minutes:seconds)
2003	Masayuki Akimoto, Japan	1:36.98	1:43.40, 1:27.06, 1:40.49
2005	Yuki Hayashi, Japan	1:04.63	1:10.31, 1:01.21, 1:02.38
2007	Mátyás Kuti, Hungary	1:02.37	1:02.78, 57.43, 1:10.36, 1:06.61, 57.71

Rubik's 4×4×4 European Champions—Past and Present

Year	European Champion	Winning Time (minutes:seconds)	All Results in Final (minutes:seconds)
2004	Olivier Gaucher, France	1:27.21	1:33.41, 1:26.80, 1:21.42
2006	Jean Pons, France	1:02.40	1:03.31, 2:05.19, 1:02.77, 57.32, 1:01.13

Rubik's 4×4×4 World Record Holders—Past and Present

Date	World Record Holder	World Record Time (minutes:seconds)
November 2007	Mátyás Kuti, Hungary	**46.63**
October 2006	Michael Fung, Netherlands	51.16
November 2005	Yuki Hayashi, Japan	54.13
August 2005	Chris Hardwick, USA	55.38
July 2005	Yuki Hayashi, Japan	1:00.38
April 2005	Frédérick Badie, France	1:01.52
January 2005	Frank Morris, USA	1:08.12
August 2004	Lars Vandenbergh, Belgium	1:09.11
August 2004	Frédérick Badie, France	1:12.49
July 2004	Chris Hardwick, USA	1:12.85

RUBIK'S PROFESSOR CUBE (5×5×5)
SPEEDCUBING FACTS AND FIGURES

Rubik's 5×5×5 World Champions—Past and Present

Year	World Champion	Winning Time (minutes:seconds)	All Results in Final (minutes:seconds)
2003	Masayuki Akimoto, Japan	2:50.45	2:56.76, 2:47.62, 2:46.96
2005	Frank Morris, USA	2:15.64	2:16.43, 2:04.03, 2:26.45
2007	Mátyás Kuti, Hungary	1:46.07	1:46.65, 1:46.78, 1:43.69,

Rubik's 5×5×5 European Champions—Past and Present

Year	European Champion	Winning Time (minutes:seconds)	All Results in Final (minutes:seconds)
2004	Lars Vandenbergh, Belgium	2:30.35	2:38.44, 2:35.53, 2:17.09
2006	Ron van Bruchem, Netherlands	2:09.57	2:08.83, 2:13.18, 2:19.48, 2:06.20, 2:06.71

Rubik's 5×5×5 World Record Holders—Past and Present

Date	World Record Holder	World Record Time (minutes:seconds)
November 2007	Mátyás Kuti, Hungary	**1:30.58**
July 2007	Takayuki Ookusa, Japan	1:38.78
February 2007	Frédérick Badie, France	1:44.47
October 2006	Frank Morris, USA	1:46.28
May 2006	Ron van Bruchem, Netherlands	1:47.22
August 2005	Frank Morris, USA	1:51.41
August 2004	Lars Vandenbergh, Belgium	2:08.45

8

SPEEDSOLVING THE CUBE

RUBIK'S MINI CUBE (2×2×2)
SPEEDCUBING FACTS AND FIGURES

Rubik's 2×2×2 World Champions—Past and Present

Year	World Champion	Winning Time (seconds)	All Results in Final (seconds)
2005	Masayuki Akimoto, Japan	8.32	10.60, 7.26, 7.71, 8.63, 8.61

Rubik's 2×2×2 European Champions—Past and Present

Year	European Champion	Winning Time (seconds)	All Results in Final (seconds)
2006	Milán Baticz, Hungary	5.92	9.48, 5.03, 5.29, 4.13, 7.45

Rubik's 2×2×2 World Record Holders—Past and Present

Date	World Record Holder	World Record Time (seconds)
November 2007	Ron von Bruchem, Netherlands	**2.65**
July 2007	Mátyás Kuti, Hungary	2.73
April 2007	Mátyás Kuti, Hungary	3.55
May 2006	Anthony Hsu, USA	3.55
December 2005	Gunnar Krig, Sweden	3.94
May 2005	Shotaro Makisumi, Japan	4.13
April 2005	Shotaro Makisumi, Japan	4.92
March 2005	Gunnar Krig, Sweden	6.35

3

Cubing Notation

Just as it is important in chess to have a notation scheme for recording the moves in a game, it is important to have a notation scheme to communicate various twists and turns of the Rubik's Cube and larger puzzles. One of the first schemes put forward was by British mathematician David Singmaster, who is also famous for the early solution described in his book, *Notes on Rubik's Magic Cube*. The notation presented in this section is based on his scheme and is the most widely accepted and used notation in speedcubing today.

This notation is used throughout this book to describe moves for the various puzzles. Please take your time to familiarize yourself with the various notational "tokens;" by doing this you will be able to make much more sense of the following chapters! You can also refer back to this section when necessary.

MOVE DESCRIPTIONS

■ **Table 3.1**
Move Notation Scheme—Uppercase Letters

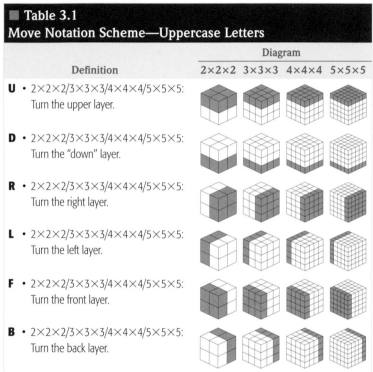

	Diagram			
Definition	2×2×2	3×3×3	4×4×4	5×5×5
U • 2×2×2/3×3×3/4×4×4/5×5×5: Turn the upper layer.				
D • 2×2×2/3×3×3/4×4×4/5×5×5: Turn the "down" layer.				
R • 2×2×2/3×3×3/4×4×4/5×5×5: Turn the right layer.				
L • 2×2×2/3×3×3/4×4×4/5×5×5: Turn the left layer.				
F • 2×2×2/3×3×3/4×4×4/5×5×5: Turn the front layer.				
B • 2×2×2/3×3×3/4×4×4/5×5×5: Turn the back layer.				

ALGORITHMS

All of the moves given in this book are described using the above notation, in strings called *algorithms*. An algorithm is a set of moves that achieves a specific effect on the cube, for example, flipping 2 edges or cycling 3 corners.

■ Table 3.2
Move Notation Scheme—Lowercase Letters

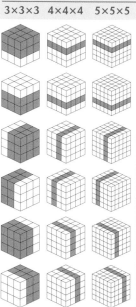

	Definition	3×3×3	4×4×4	5×5×5
u	• 3×3×3: Turn the upper 2 layers. • 4×4×4/5×5×5: Turn the inner-upper layer.			
d	• 3×3×3: Turn the "down" 2 layers. • 4×4×4/5×5×5: Turn the inner-down layer.			
r	• 3×3×3: Turn the right 2 layers. • 4×4×4/5×5×5: Turn the inner-right layer.			
l	• 3×3×3: Turn the left 2 layers. • 4×4×4/5×5×5: Turn the inner-left layer.			
f	• 3×3×3: Turn the front 2 layers. • 4×4×4/5×5×5: Turn the inner-front layer.			
b	• 3×3×3: Turn the back 2 layers. • 4×4×4/5×5×5: Turn the inner-back layer.			

■ Table 3.3
Move Notation Scheme—Special Symbols

	Special symbols indicating directionality or other information
	No symbol means a clockwise turn of a face or rotation of the cube.
'	This symbol describes a counterclockwise turn of a face or rotation of the cube.
2	This symbol describes a 180° clockwise turn of a face or rotation of the cube.
2'	This symbol describes a 180° counterclockwise turn of a face or rotation of the cube.
*	This symbol indicates that the moves within the preceding brackets are to be executed a multiple number of times.

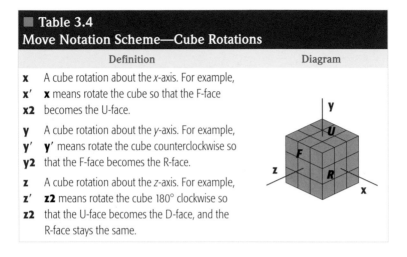

■ Table 3.4
Move Notation Scheme—Cube Rotations

Definition	Diagram
x A cube rotation about the *x*-axis. For example, **x′** **x** means rotate the cube so that the F-face **x2** becomes the U-face.	
y A cube rotation about the *y*-axis. For example, **y′** **y′** means rotate the cube counterclockwise so **y2** that the F-face becomes the R-face.	
z A cube rotation about the *z*-axis. For example, **z′** **z2** means rotate the cube 180° clockwise so **z2** that the U-face becomes the D-face, and the R-face stays the same.	

■ Example

A well-known **algorithm** among speedcubers is the "Sune." First named by Swedish speedcuber Lars Petrus, this algorithm twists 3 corners (and also repositions some pieces). Written in cubing notation, the algorithm is:

R U R′ U R U2 R′

How do we interpret this?

The first letter is **R**. There is no symbol after, such as a ′ or a 2, so the first turn is the right layer 90° clockwise. Second is **U**, again with no symbol, so the next turn is the upper layer 90° clockwise. Third we have **R** again, this time combined with the ′ symbol, so we must turn the right layer 90° counterclockwise. Continue through to the end of the algorithm, and if you have performed it correctly, it will have the desired effect on your cube.

DESCRIBING THE LAYERS, FACES, PIECES, AND STICKERS

When talking about cubes, it is useful to be able to quickly refer to different aspects such as a layer, a face, a piece, or a sticker. The layers and faces are straightforward; they work in the same way as the move notation, so the upper layer is called the U-layer, the right face is called the R-face, and so forth.

When describing pieces, or positions of pieces, we use a combination of letters that describes the layers the piece is on.

To talk about stickers, we use the same notation, but the **first** letter also tells us which face the sticker is on. So if we talk about the URF piece in Figure 3.1, we are referring to the whole corner piece, but if we talk about the URF sticker, we are referring to the Yellow sticker only—it is on the U-face and belongs to the corner piece that is at URF.

This notational system works for all of the different sizes of cubes. Each piece is described in the same way.

Figure 3.2 shows some examples of possible 4×4×4 pieces. The Red/Yellow edge piece is at UFr, or FUr, or any such combination of those 3 letters, because it makes up part of the r-layer, the U-layer, and the F-layer simultaneously. If we want to talk about the Red

Figure 3.1 The position of the Red/Yellow/Green corner is known as the URF position, or FRU position, or RUF position, because it is at the intersection of the U-layer, R-layer, and F-layer. The position of the White/Blue edge is known as the FR or RF position, because it is at the intersection of the F-layer and R-layer.

Figure 3.2

sticker of the Red/Yellow edge, we describe it as the FUr sticker—the F comes first since the Red sticker is on the F-face. Similarly, the Red/Green edge is described as being at uRF, FRu, and so forth, but the Red sticker would always be described as the FRu sticker. The Red center piece is at Fur, because it is on the F-face and makes up part of both the u-layer and the r-layer.

Figure 3.3 shows some examples of possible 5×5×5 pieces that we might want to describe. The pieces that are dead center of each face (that is, the Red and Yellow dead centers) are simply known as the center pieces. To describe the Yellow center that is diagonally across from dead center, we say that it is in the Ubr position, because it is on the U-face and makes up part of both the b-layer and the r-layer. The other pieces in the diagram are named Fr, UF, FRU, and UFr—see if you can match the names with the pieces.

Figure 3.3

INVERSES OF ALGORITHMS

The same algorithm can be inverted to achieve a similar but different effect on the cube. For example, the inverse of an algorithm that cycles 3 edges clockwise will cycle 3 edges counterclockwise.

Inverting an algorithm is easy; just read it backward and change the directional symbols. So where you see no symbol, replace it with a ′; where you see a ′, remove it; and where you see a **2**, leave it alone (or replace it with a **2′**).

For example, the inverse of **R′ F R′ B2 R F′ R′ B2 R2** is **R2 B2 R F R′ B2 R F′ R**.

If you perform an algorithm, and then its inverse, you get back to the original state.

Don't worry if the notation seems a little confusing at first; just read through it a couple of times, and it will begin to make perfect sense. I promise.

4 A Beginner's Method for Solving the 3×3×3 Rubik's Cube

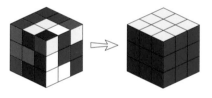

For a lot of people, just being able to solve the cube is satisfying enough, which is absolutely fine. But speaking from personal experience as a speedcuber, simply being able to solve Rubik's Cube is **not** enough; solving it as fast as possible is the exciting part! In the following tutorials, I present a wealth of information focused on **first enabling you to solve Rubik's Cube** and then helping you to **improve your solving times by teaching you some more advanced speedcubing techniques**. Think of it as first learning to drive and then training to become a Formula 1 racing driver.

Unofficially, some people say that you become a speedcuber once you can solve Rubik's Cube in under 60 seconds. Other people say that the only qualification required to be a speedcuber is that you race the clock while solving your cube. The 60-second barrier is very possible to achieve even with the beginner solution. At first it may take you several minutes to solve a cube, but as with any skill, practice is the key, and you will soon be dramatically improving your times.

The world's elite can solve the puzzle in an average time of less than 20 seconds, and these days averages of under 15 seconds are becoming increasingly common. By learning the advanced solution and absorbing some of the expert techniques that I describe in chapters 5 and 6, you will be well on your way to joining the elite ranks. But you cannot do it without a lot of practice and dedication.

However far you want to get in the world of speedcubing, whether it is just being able to solve the cube to show off to your friends or becoming the world champion, this book is here to help you. Good luck!

THINGS TO KNOW BEFORE YOU GET STARTED

If you haven't already read the chapter about cubing notation (chapter 3), please do so now. Unless you are familiar with the notation, this tutorial will not make much sense to you. Don't worry, the notation is very simple and fairly intuitive, and it will not take many minutes of your time to learn it.

The Rubik's Cube has 6 faces, and when the puzzle is solved, each face will be a single, unique color. The majority of Rubik's Cubes possess the "BOY" color scheme, where Red is opposite Orange, Blue opposite Green, and Yellow opposite White. There will also be a corner piece that is Blue/Orange/Yellow, reading clockwise.

When you first look at the cube, you may notice that there are 54 individual colored stickers, 9 on each face. Stop right there! Rather than viewing the cube this way, look at it as **26 separate blocks**, known as "cubies," instead. You can never separate the colors on a single cubie, no matter how hard you try, because they are, of course, fixed. There are **12 edge cubies**, which have 2 stickers each, **8 corner cubies**, which have 3 stickers each, and **6 center cubies**, each with 1 sticker. The center cubies are fixed in position relative to each other by the 6-armed core mechanism inside the cube. This means the center cubie determines the color of the whole face. For example, if your cube has a Red center **opposite** an Orange center, it would be a waste of time attempting to build a Red face **next** to an Orange face, because the centers are fixed.

There are an amazing 43,252,003,274,489,856,000 possible configurations of Rubik's Cube, and only 1 of them is the solved position! That's **43 quintillion, 252 quadrillion, 3 trillion, 274 billion, 489 million, 856 thousand!** It's not necessary to know this in order to solve it, but it is interesting to find out where this number comes from.

Now that you are familiar with some of the basic knowledge needed to solve the cube, you're ready to go on and attempt it.

Number of Positions of Rubik's Cube

There are 6 centers that can take 1 possible arrangement (since they are fixed and exclude rotations); 8 corners, each of which have 3 possible orientations and 8 possible positions; and 12 edges, each of which have 2 possible orientations and 12 possible positions. This gives us a number of configurations:

$$3^8 \times 8! \times 2^{12} \times 12!$$

However, we have to put a few restrictions in place on this number. If 7 of the corners are twisted in position randomly, the orientation of the eighth corner is predetermined. This means we must divide by 3. Similarly, if 11 of the edges are randomly flipped, the orientation of the twelfth edge is fixed, meaning we further divide by 2. Finally, we cannot swap pieces an odd number of times. This means if we swap the positions of 2 corner pieces, then 2 edges must swap as well, or another 2 corners must be swapped. It is impossible to swap a single pair of pieces, and the consequence is that half of these positions cannot be reached.

The final number of configurations is:

$$\frac{3^8 \times 8! \times 2^{12} \times 12!}{3 \times 2 \times 2}$$

which equals:

43,252,003,274,489,856,000

THE BEGINNER METHOD

The initial step on the road to becoming a speedcuber is by far the hardest and most frustrating. As a beginner, with no experience using a predefined strategy to solve Rubik's Cube, you have a lot of obstacles to overcome and mountains to climb before you reach your first goal—solving your cube!

Be patient, be determined, and don't give up. The satisfaction and triumph of solving your first cube is something that cannot be described; you must experience it for yourself. It has to be said, however, that you will get a lot more satisfaction if you have already made a concerted effort to solve the cube by yourself, before seeking assistance. Once you have learned to solve the cube, you can never really unlearn it. By giving yourself a chance to succeed on your own at this stage, you'll be much more proud of the end result. Solving the cube on one's own is not something that everyone can achieve—even I couldn't manage to figure out the last stages by myself and had to seek help—so it's **definitely not** something to be ashamed of or an indication that you don't have the necessary intelligence to ever solve it.

The General Strategy

The beginner method presented on the next few pages is known as a "layer-by-layer" solution. First of all, we will solve the bottom (down) layer in 2 steps, and then we'll proceed to solve the middle layer. We'll finish off the cube by solving the top (up) layer in 4 stages, treating the position and orientation of the corners and edges separately in each stage. Once we have completed all 3 layers, the cube is solved!

Solving the First Layer Edges

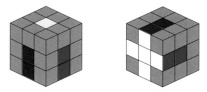

This step is probably the hardest of them all because you must first overcome the hurdle of having no experience with the cube, and you have the freedom of the whole cube in which to move pieces around. There are no easy fixes; you just have to "see" it.

Start off by selecting a color that will be your "bottom face color." I always select White, for reasons I discuss in chapter 6, but for the layer-by-layer method, it doesn't matter which color you start with. It may feel more natural for you to start solving the top layer first, and at this stage it doesn't matter where you position your first layer. When you begin to get faster and progress to more advanced systems, you will see how solving the bottom layer first can be a big advantage.

Hold your cube with your chosen bottom face color on the bottom, and try to keep it on the bottom at all times. This will make it easier for you at these early stages, but once you get more used to the cube, this won't be so important. There are 4 edge pieces (the pieces with 2 stickers) that have a sticker of the same color as your bottom face color, and we will focus on solving these pieces first.

Look first in the top layer for these edge pieces, because these are easier to solve than edge pieces that may be stuck in the middle layer. When there are no more pieces of the bottom face color in the top layer, search in the middle layer and finally in the bottom layer. Table 4.1 shows you what to do for each case.

■ **Table 4.1**
3×3×3 Beginner Method—First Layer Edges

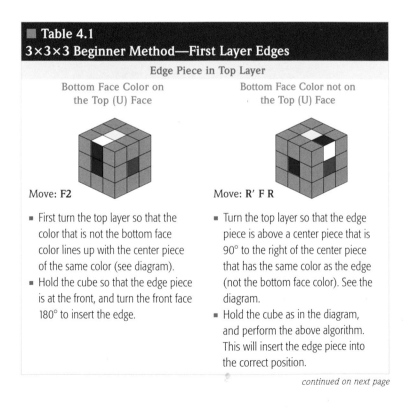

Edge Piece in Top Layer	
Bottom Face Color on the Top (U) Face	Bottom Face Color not on the Top (U) Face
Move: **F2**	Move: **R' F R**
■ First turn the top layer so that the color that is not the bottom face color lines up with the center piece of the same color (see diagram).	■ Turn the top layer so that the edge piece is above a center piece that is 90° to the right of the center piece that has the same color as the edge (not the bottom face color). See the diagram.
■ Hold the cube so that the edge piece is at the front, and turn the front face 180° to insert the edge.	■ Hold the cube as in the diagram, and perform the above algorithm. This will insert the edge piece into the correct position.

continued on next page

continued from previous page

Edge Piece in Middle or Bottom Layer

Edge Piece in Middle Layer	Edge Piece in Bottom Layer
Move: **R U R'**	Move: **R2**

- Hold the cube so that the edge is at the front-right (FR) position (see diagram).
- Apply the above algorithm to displace the edge piece from the middle layer and place it in the top layer.
- Now you have 1 of the "edge piece in top layer" cases, which are described above.

- Hold the cube so that the edge is at the bottom-right position (see diagram).
- Apply the above algorithm to displace the edge piece from the bottom layer, and place it into the top layer.
- Now you have 1 of the "edge piece in top layer" cases, which are described above.

When you solve these pieces, you must make sure that the edge sticker with the bottom face color is placed on the bottom and that the other color on the edge piece matches up with a center piece of the same color. The edge must have both colors matching the respective center pieces; otherwise, you will never end up with a solved cube.

With a little bit of practice, once you have applied the above moves as necessary to all 4 edge pieces, you will have solved the bottom layer edges. Congratulations! Your cube should look something like Figure 4.1; however, you may have chosen a different bottom face color than White. The most important thing to notice is how the colors on the bottom edges match those of the center pieces.

Out of all the stages outlined in this beginner method, this first step requires the most intuition. Be patient and take some time to get to know the various cases. Believe me, with practice it becomes very easy! Once you have mastered this step, you are ready to solve the first layer corners.

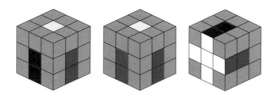

Figure 4.1 A solved White cross

Solving the First Layer Corners

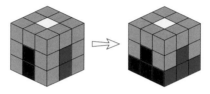

When solving the first layer corners, we will continue to hold the cube so that our bottom face color is on the bottom. There are 4 corner pieces that have a sticker of the same color as your bottom face color, and we will now focus on these corner pieces.

As before, start searching for these pieces in the top layer, and once you have exhausted the supply of top layer corner pieces, continue your search in the bottom layer (of course, corner pieces cannot possibly be in the middle layer). Continue until you have solved all 4 corners and you obtain a completed first layer.

To identify where a corner piece should go in the first layer, look at the other 2 colors (not the bottom face color). The corner piece will go in the bottom layer, between the 2 center pieces that have these colors.

Table 4.2 shows all the possible cases you will encounter and what to do for each.

Once you have solved all 4 corners, you will have completed the first layer. In fact, you are ⅓ of the way to solving the entire cube! Practice by solving the first layer many times, and it won't be long before you completely

■ Table 4.2
3×3×3 Beginner Method—First Layer Corners

Unsolved Corner Piece in Top Layer

Bottom Face Color on Front	Bottom Face Color on Right	Bottom Face Color on Top
Move: F' U' F	Move: R U R'	Move: R U2 R'

- Turn the top layer to position the corner piece directly above the position in which it belongs (see diagram).
- Apply the above algorithm to insert the corner piece correctly into the first layer.

- Turn the top layer to position the corner piece directly above the position in which it belongs (see diagram).
- Applying the above algorithm changes the case into the "bottom face color on right" case, which you can then solve.

Unsolved Corner Piece in Bottom Layer

Move: R U R'

- Hold the cube so that the corner piece is at the bottom right (see diagram).
- Apply the above algorithm to move the corner piece into the top layer. You can then use 1 of the above tricks to move the corner piece into its correct position.

master this step. When you are able to solve the first layer every time, you are ready to move on to the second layer.

Solving the Second Layer

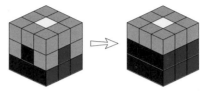

If you have managed to make it this far, solving the second layer will seem relatively straightforward. As with the previous steps, continue to hold the cube so that your bottom face color (the completed first layer) remains on the bottom.

To complete the second layer, which will be the middle layer, you must place 4 edges into their correct positions. You can identify these edges in the top or middle layers if their sticker colors **are not** the same color as the top center piece. We will focus on these 4 edges during this part of the solution, but we must be careful not to mess up what we have already solved.

The second layer can mostly be solved by applying just 1 simple procedure; however, some special cases crop up now and again. All the moves you need to know are detailed in Table 4.3.

Carry on applying the appropriate algorithms until the middle layer is solved. Once all 4 edges are in position, you are ⅔ of the way to completing the cube! With a little practice, you will see that solving the middle layer is simply a case of repeating the same movements over and over again. Once you've got the hang of these algorithms, you will be able to successfully complete the middle layer 100% of the time. As soon as you feel comfortable solving the first and second layers (known collectively as the "first 2 layers," or "F2L"), you can move on to solving the last layer and with it, the whole cube.

■ Table 4.3
3×3×3 Beginner Method—Solving the Second Layer

Middle Layer Edge Piece in Top Layer

Edge Piece Belongs in Front-Right Position	Edge Piece Belongs in Front-Left Position
Move: **U R U′ R′ F R′ F′ R**	Move: **U′ L′ U L F′ L F L′**

- Identify the color of the edge sticker around the side of the U-layer, and turn the U-layer to line up that sticker with its matching center color. Hold the edge so it is on the **front** face (see diagrams).
- Identify which position you need to move the edge into (either the left or right), and apply the appropriate algorithm detailed above.

Middle Layer Edge Piece in Middle Layer

Occasionally you will find no more solvable edges in the top layer, yet the middle layer is incomplete. This can happen when 2 middle layer edge pieces are swapped over, or if a middle layer edge is in the correct position but the colors are flipped over.

Move: **U R U′ R′ F R′ F′ R**

- Hold the cube so that 1 of the wrong edges is at the front-right position (see diagram).
- Apply the above algorithm, which will place a random piece from the top layer into the middle layer, and the edge piece that was in the middle layer will now be in the top layer. You can then use 1 of the "middle layer edge piece in top layer" tricks to solve it.

Solving the Last Layer

By the time you reach the last layer, you will by definition have completed the first 2 layers. This means that there are only 8 more pieces to solve, but it also means that you have much less freedom in which to manipulate the pieces, because you must be careful to keep the piece positions you have already solved.

I will present 2 methods for solving the last layer; the first, known as the "EZ" LL, allows you to solve the last layer with as few algorithms as possible. After that, I will show you other algorithms that allow you to take care of each of the 4 last layer steps more efficiently.

Flip the Last Layer Edges (Form a Cross on Top)

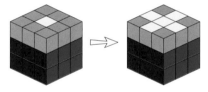

The goal of this step is to flip, or "orient," the top layer edges correctly. The end result will be the formation of a cross on the top of your cube (see diagram above). Unlike the cross we formed at the beginning of the solution, it doesn't matter at this stage if some of the colors around the side of the layer do not match up; we will take care of those in a later step.

A physical constraint of Rubik's Cube is that edge pieces can only be flipped in pairs. This restricts the number of possible cases you will encounter at this stage. Since edge pieces are flipped only in pairs, you can flip 4, 2, or 0 edges. If you encounter a position in which you have to flip an odd number of edges, it means that at some point your cube broke apart and was reassembled incorrectly. To fix this, you must break it apart again and flip over 1 edge to restore "even parity," since no sequence of moves can flip just 1 edge.

To flip the top layer edges to form a cross pattern on the top, first identify which case you have from the table below. Hold the cube so that it matches the diagram, and apply the appropriate algorithms from either Table 4.4a (the "EZ" way) or Table 4.4b (the more efficient way).

Position the Final Layer Edges

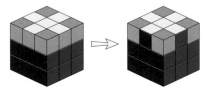

Now that all the top layer edges are oriented correctly, we need to move them into their correct positions. This is called "permuting" the top layer edges.

First of all, make sure to check that this step is necessary! In some cases, the edges will already be correctly permuted, so you can skip this step and move immediately to the next. If you can turn the top layer such that all the edge colors match with the center piece colors, then the edges are correctly permuted.

Most of the time, however, it is necessary to permute the edges. For an easy way to solve the edges from here, check out the procedure in Table 4.5a (the "EZ" way), or if you want a more efficient way of permuting the edges, look at Table 4.5b.

The algorithms in Table 4.5a are examples of inverse processes. The algorithm to permute the edges counterclockwise is simply the algorithm to permute the edges clockwise read backward. Both of the algorithms are known as "order 3" algorithms, meaning that if you perform the move 3 times, you get back to the position you started with. It is therefore possible to learn only 1 of these moves, and when you encounter the other case, you simply apply the move you have learned twice instead of once. It is up to you how much you want to learn at this stage.

Table 4.4a
3×3×3 Beginner Method—Solving the Last Layer ("EZ" Way)

Flip the Top Layer Edges Correctly (Top Color = Yellow).

Move: **F R U R′ U′ F′ U**

Keep applying the above algorithm to your cube until you reach the position shown in the diagram. It is possible that you will reach a position where the Yellow edges are at UF and UB; in this case, it is obvious (I hope!) that you just do **U** to arrive at the position shown in the diagram.

Once you have arrived at this position, apply the algorithm once more to flip the top layer edges correctly.

Table 4.4b
3×3×3 Beginner Method—Solving the Last Layer (More Efficient Way)

Flip the Top Layer Edges Correctly (Top Color = Yellow).

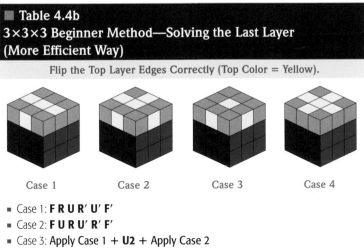

| Case 1 | Case 2 | Case 3 | Case 4 |

- Case 1: **F R U R′ U′ F′**
- Case 2: **F U R U′ R′ F′**
- Case 3: Apply Case 1 + **U2** + Apply Case 2
- Case 4: You already have a cross on top. Continue to the next step.

■ Table 4.5a
3×3×3 Beginner Method—Solving the Last Layer ("EZ" Way)

Permute the top layer edges correctly (top color = Yellow).

Move: **R U2 R′ U′ R U′ R′**

Try to position your last layer so that 1 edge and 1 edge only is solved. If this is possible, hold the cube so that the solved edge is at the front, and apply the above algorithm. You may have to apply it 1 or 2 times, depending on the situation. If you cannot position your last layer so that only 1 edge is solved, just apply the above algorithm and then try again.

By now you should have completely solved the top layer edges. All that remains to solve are the top layer corners, discussed in the next 2 sections.

Twist the Final Layer Corners

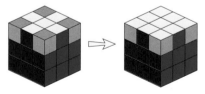

The penultimate step in the solution is to twist, or "orient," the final layer corners. After you have completed this step successfully, the top face will be solved, but not the top layer. **Be very careful with this step;** it is easy to get wrong, and if you do so, you will end up back at square 1!

■ Table 4.5b
3×3×3 Beginner Method—Solving the Last Layer
(More Efficient Way)

Permute the top layer edges correctly (top color = Yellow).

Permute Edges Clockwise

Permute Edges Counterclockwise

Move: **R U2 R′ U′ R U′ R′**

Move: **R U R′ U R U2 R′**

Adjacent Edge Swap

Move: **R U2 R′ U′ R U′ R′ 1 U2 1 R U R′ U R U2 R′**

Try to position your last layer so that only 1 edge is solved. Hold the solved edge at the front, and apply 1 of the moves from the top 2 diagrams, depending on how you need to cycle around the edges. If you cannot position the last layer so that only 1 edge is solved, you must perform an adjacent edge swap, which is really just a combination of clockwise and counterclockwise 3-edge cycles.

During each iteration of the process, you will orient the corner that is in the top-right-back position, so when starting with this step, make sure you hold the cube so that a wrongly twisted corner is in this position. The "EZ" way is shown in Table 4.6a, and the more efficient method is shown in Table 4.6b.

It will probably take you a few attempts to get this process correct, and it will be frustrating. But be patient, because once you get the knack, it will

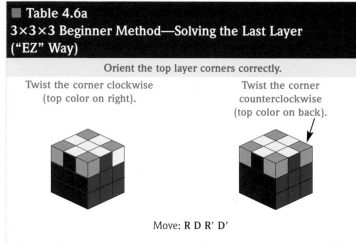

■ **Table 4.6a**
3×3×3 Beginner Method—Solving the Last Layer ("EZ" Way)

Orient the top layer corners correctly.

Twist the corner clockwise (top color on right).

Twist the corner counterclockwise (top color on back).

Move: **R D R' D'**

Turn the U-layer so that an unoriented corner is at UBR (see diagrams). Apply the move above as many times as necessary to bring the correct sticker to the upper layer (in this case, the Yellow sticker).

Next, don't rotate the cube, but turn the U-layer to bring the next unoriented corner into the UBR position, and repeat the procedure. Continue to do this until all corners are correctly twisted. Don't worry about the first 2 layers becoming a mess; it will be restored once you have correctly oriented all the corners.

become straightforward to perform. All that remains now is to position the final layer corners and finish off the cube!

Position the Final Layer Corners

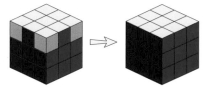

The final step in the solution is to position, or "permute," the final layer corners. First you must identify a corner that is already solved (read on for what to do if this is not the case). This corner is easy to see; it will

■ Table 4.6b
3×3×3 Beginner Method—Solving the Last Layer
(More Efficient Way)

Orient the top layer corners correctly.

Twist the corner clockwise (top color on right).	Twist the corner counterclockwise (top color on back).
Move: **R D R′ D′ R D R′ D′**	Move: **D R D′ R′ D R D′ R′**

- Identify which of the cases you have at the beginning, and apply the appropriate algorithm to twist the corner correctly. When it is correctly twisted, the top layer color will be on the top face.
- *Stop!* Each algorithm twists an individual corner on the top face and also appears to randomize the bottom layer somewhat, so it will appear that all the hard work put in at the beginning of the solve has been undone. But **don't worry,** it's supposed to be like this! *Don't rotate the cube in your hands,* but turn the top layer to move the next incorrect corner into the back-right position. Again select the appropriate algorithm from the ones above, and when you have corrected all of the incorrectly twisted corners, the top face should be solved, *and* the first 2 layers will be magically restored!

be the only corner piece around which all the stickers match up perfectly, just as they do when the cube is in the solved state. Once you have identified this corner, follow the procedure described in Table 4.7a or Table 4.7b to finish off your cube.

Don't be put off by the length of these algorithms. They are simply a combination of 2 "substeps" to achieve an effect on the cube. The moves enclosed in parentheses are the same substep; the only difference

■ Table 4.7a
3×3×3 Beginner Method—Solving the Last Layer
("EZ" Way)

Permute the top layer corners correctly.

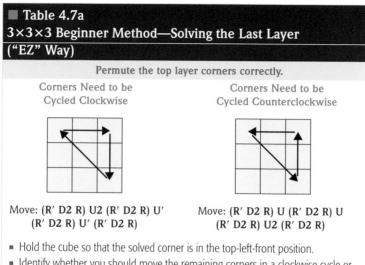

Corners Need to be Cycled Clockwise	Corners Need to be Cycled Counterclockwise
Move: (R' D2 R) U2 (R' D2 R) U' (R' D2 R) U' (R' D2 R)	Move: (R' D2 R) U (R' D2 R) U (R' D2 R) U2 (R' D2 R)

- Hold the cube so that the solved corner is in the top-left-front position.
- Identify whether you should move the remaining corners in a clockwise cycle or a counterclockwise cycle. You can discover this by working out where the corner piece in the top-right-front position needs to be, and then working out where the corner in *that* position needs to be, and so on. You will trace out either a clockwise or a counterclockwise cycle.
- Apply the appropriate move from the selection above.

is how you turn the top layer, and this should be easy to understand, even without learning the algorithm.

The first step is to place the corner that was in the top-right-front position into the down-back-left position, using the algorithm **R' D2 R**. Next, look for the position where the corner piece, now in the down-back-left position, should go. In the case of the clockwise corner cycle, the down-back-left corner belongs in the top-back-left. So we turn the top layer to bring the corner in this position to the top-front-right (**U2**), and we again swap this with the down-back-left corner (**R' D2 R**). By doing this, we solve the corner that was in the down-back-left position, and we have replaced it with another corner piece to solve. By repeating

■ **Table 4.7b**
3×3×3 Beginner Method—Solving the Last Layer (More Efficient Way)

Permute the top layer corners correctly.

Corners Need to be Cycled Clockwise	Corners Need to be Cycled Counterclockwise
Move: **(x) R′ U R′ D2 R U′ R′ D2 R2**	Move: **(x) R2 D2 R U R′ D2 R U′ R**

- Hold the cube so that the solved corner is in the top-left-front position.
- Identify whether you need to move the remaining corners in a clockwise cycle or a counterclockwise cycle. You can discover this by working out where the corner piece in the top-right-front position needs to be, and then working out where the corner in *that* position needs to be, and so on. You will trace out either a clockwise or a counterclockwise cycle.
- Apply the appropriate move from the selection above.

this process, all the corners will eventually end up in their correct positions, and the top layer will be solved! However, if you want more direct algorithms, check out Table 4.7b.

But what if we don't have 1 solved corner to begin with? There are 2 possible cases where this can occur, and 2 reasonable ways to take care of it. We can use the same tactic we used when it wasn't possible to solve only 1 edge in the "permute final layer edges" step, or we can learn a completely separate algorithm. Both scenarios are described in Table 4.8 below.

Again, don't be put off by the length of the first algorithms; they work on exactly the same principle as before, swapping corners from

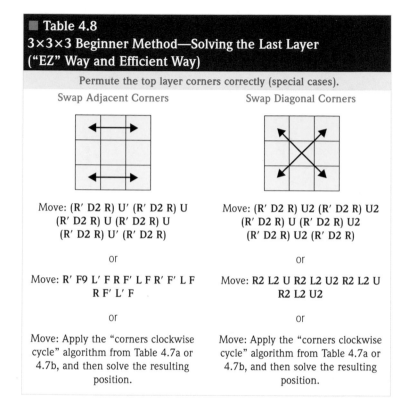

■ Table 4.8
3×3×3 Beginner Method—Solving the Last Layer
("EZ" Way and Efficient Way)

Permute the top layer corners correctly (special cases).

Swap Adjacent Corners	Swap Diagonal Corners
Move: (R′ D2 R) U′ (R′ D2 R) U (R′ D2 R) U (R′ D2 R) U (R′ D2 R) U′ (R′ D2 R)	Move: (R′ D2 R) U2 (R′ D2 R) U2 (R′ D2 R) U (R′ D2 R) U2 (R′ D2 R) U2 (R′ D2 R)
or	or
Move: R′ F9 L′ F R F′ L F R′ F′ L F R F′ L′ F	Move: R2 L2 U R2 L2 U2 R2 L2 U R2 L2 U2
or	or
Move: Apply the "corners clockwise cycle" algorithm from Table 4.7a or 4.7b, and then solve the resulting position.	Move: Apply the "corners clockwise cycle" algorithm from Table 4.7a or 4.7b, and then solve the resulting position.

the top layer with the corner in the down-back-left position until all the corners are in their correct positions.

Now that the top layer is finished, line it up with the first 2 layers and *voila*, you have solved your first cube! Congratulations on making it this far; it is just a matter of practice before you can solve the cube without any assistance from this book. But this is only the beginning. Now that you have learned how to solve the cube, simply solving it is not enough—you have to solve it as fast as possible! Using the method described in this chapter, it is possible to get times down to around 45 to 50 seconds. To get faster, you must use a more advanced, and more complicated, method. One of the best and most widely used methods for speedcubing is known as the "Fridrich" system, described in detail in chapter 5.

Beginner Method Example Scrambles and Solutions

Start with a solved cube and apply the scramble algorithm with your chosen bottom face color on the bottom. Be sure to apply the scramble correctly; otherwise, the solution won't make very much sense. Use the images in Table 4.9 as a guide only. If you scramble with Red on front and Yellow on up, then your cube should look like the diagram after scrambling. If you scramble with any other orientation, or you have a different color scheme, then it won't match the diagram exactly, but the pattern of colors should be the same.

■ Table 4.9
Beginner Method—Example Solutions

Example Scramble 1: U2 L B2 F2 L′ D2 L2 D′ B′ R′ B F2 R′ B2
F2 D2 U L2 R U′ F D′ U F2 L2

Solving the first layer edges:

- **y U F2**
- **R2 y′ U2 F2**
- **y′ U F2**
- **y R U R′ y2 U R′ F R**

Solving the first layer corners:

- **U2 R U2 R′ U′ R U R′**
- **y2 U F′ U′ F**
- **y′ U R U R′**
- **y2 R U2 R′ U′ R U R′**

Solving the second layer:

- **y2 U′ L′ U L F′ L F L′**
- **y2 U2 U R U′ R′ F R′ F′ R**
- **U2 U′ L′ U L F′ L F L′**

Solving the final layer:

- **y F R U R′ U′ F′**—Orient the edges.
- **y′ R U2 R′ U′ R U′ R′**—Permute the edges.
- **y2 (R D R′ D′ R D R′ D′) U′ (D R D′ R′ D R D′ R′)**—Orient the corners.
- **U**—Line up the layers; solved!

Example Scramble 2: L B2 F D' B F' L2 B2 F2 L B' F L2 B'
F' R D' U' F U' F D2 B' F2 U'

Solving the first layer edges:
- **y2 U R' F R**
- **R U R' U L2**
- **B2**
- **y U R' F R**

Solving the first layer corners:
- **y2 U2 R U R'**
- **y' R U2 R' U' R U R'**
- **y2 U2 F' U' F**
- **y R U R'**

Solving the second layer:
- **y2 U' L' U L F' L F L'**
- **U U R U' R' F R' F' R**
- **y2 U2 U' L' U L F' L F L'**

Solving the final layer:
- **F R U R' U' F'**–Orient the edges.
- **R U2 R' U' R U' R' y2 R U R' U R U2 R'**–Permute the edges (note we had to use the tactic of performing the move twice this time).
- **y2 (R D R' D' R D R' D')** U' **(D R D' R' D R D' R')**–Orient the corners.
- **U y** (lining up the solved corner) **(R' D2 R) U2 (R' D2 R) U' (R' D2 R) U' (R' D2 R)**–Permute the corners.

5 A Speedcubing Method for Solving the 3×3×3 Rubik's Cube

I n this chapter I present a wealth of information about an advanced speedcubing method known as the CFOP system, which is the system I currently use for speedcubing. This method has allowed me to set personal-best average times of under 15 seconds.

INTRODUCTION TO THE CFOP SYSTEM

The CFOP system is a very efficient layer-by-layer solution that enables speedcubers to solve Rubik's Cube in under 20 seconds on average. CFOP stands for **C**ross, **F**irst 2 Layers, **O**rient Last Layer, and **P**ermute Last Layer, which describe the various steps of the system in the order that they are applied. It is widely accepted that Jessica Fridrich of the Czech Republic was the first speedcuber to realize the potential of this powerful system. The ideas for solving the first 2 layers simultaneously had already been documented, but she is credited with the inspirational idea in 1981 of solving the last layer in 2 steps instead of 4 steps, which was commonplace at the time. She notes on her website that her first realization of such a system came when a friend mentioned on a particular cube-solving occasion, "Oh, I like this 'T' pattern, because when you turn the edges, the whole last layer will actually flip correctly."

A 1982 World Championship finalist, Fridrich was also the first person to document this method for solving Rubik's Cube on the Internet, when she set up her speedcubing page in 1997. Without her effort, it is very likely that speedcubing as it is known today would never have come into existence. It is for this that she will be forever associated with the CFOP system, which is also known worldwide as the Fridrich system.

It is worth mentioning that other methods exist that are also extremely fast and efficient. One such system is the Petrus method, invented by 1982 World Championship finalist Lars Petrus of Sweden. The Petrus method starts by making a 2×2×2 block, expanding this to a 2×2×3, fixing "bad edges" (edges not correctly oriented within a 2-generator reference frame), and then solving the rest. Petrus claims the advantage of this method is that, unlike layer-by-layer solutions, you never break up and restore parts of the cube you have already solved in order to solve further parts.

Another very quick system is the Roux method, invented by Frenchman Gilles Roux, who is also the 2006 European Fewest Moves Champion. In his system, you first build a 1×2×3 block and then a 1×2×3 block on the opposite side. You continue by solving the 4 remaining corners, and then finish off the 6 remaining edges. This solution is extremely efficient in terms of numbers of moves, but it requires a lot of insight and intuition. There are also various fast "corners first" methods, one of which is known as the Waterman method, but none of these methods have matched the popularity of the CFOP system. I wish you every success in your quest to learn this method and to make the transition from cubing to speedcubing!

The General Strategy

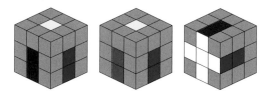

As with the beginner solution, the first step is to make a cross shape on the bottom face. However, in this section I go into a lot more depth about solving the cross, and I introduce some techniques that will be useful only if you already have experience solving the cube using the beginner solution. Then we'll continue by solving the corners of the bottom layer and the edges of the middle layer simultaneously, known collectively as the "first 2 layers." Finally, we'll finish the cube by first solving the top face and then solving the top layer. Each step requires quite a bit more memorization that any step in the beginner solution, but by learning it a step at a time, it will not be long before you are familiar with most, if not all, of the algorithms.

Solving the Cross

The first step is to locate and solve the 4 edge pieces that make up the cross. This Cross step is so called because when the first 4 edge pieces are solved, a cross pattern is formed on 1 of the faces. This is an intuitive step and requires no memorization of algorithms, but it does require 100% concentration!

Solving the cross quickly and efficiently is a real art form, and you can learn it only through practice and experience. Unlike the beginner solution to the cross, where we solved the 4 cross edges independently, we now must attempt to solve all 4 edges simultaneously. A beginner cannot pick up the cube and expect to see the optimal solution to the cross straightaway (a lot of experts have trouble with this, too), let alone execute it in the best way. The top speedcubers aim to solve the cross in around 2 seconds or less.

In this section, I explain and demonstrate some of the things you should look for during your pre-inspection of the cube, along with some tricks and techniques that you can learn. I also give examples for various cases, with explanations of the ideas behind the solution. Keep practicing, but don't expect to master it in 1 day.

Computer analysis by 2004 European speedcubing champion Lars Vandenbergh of Belgium has shown that from every possible starting configuration, there is an optimal solution of **8 moves or less** (see Table 5.1).

Important points to note are that almost all (> 99.9%) cases can be solved in 7 moves or less, and on most occasions you require only 5 or

■ Table 5.1
3×3×3 Advanced Method—Cross Statistics

# Moves to Solve	# Cases (out of 190,080)	% of Total Cases	Cumulative %
0	1	0.00005	< 0.1
1	15	0.008	< 0.1
2	158	0.08	< 0.1
3	1,394	0.7	0.8
4	9,809	5.2	6.0
5	46,381	24.4	30.4
6	97,254	51.2	81.6
7	34,966	18.4	> 99.9
8	102	0.05	100

6 moves to solve the cross. Therefore, if you could see the shortest or near shortest cross solution every time, and execute it quickly, a cross in 1.5 to 2 seconds is perfectly reasonable.

Some Initial Advice

My first and foremost recommendation is to **always solve the cross on the bottom face**. If your current method is to make a cross on the top face, and then turn the cube upside down at some stage to solve the final layers, I recommend that you get out of this habit immediately. A few speedcubers prefer to solve the cross on the left, which is possibly just as good as solving the cross on the bottom, but I shall concentrate on "cross on bottom" solving since this is the method I like best and find easiest to use. Solving with the cross on the bottom is a good idea; it allows you to have the **best view of the U-layer**, which means that you can easily look ahead and search for the F2L pieces while you solve the cross. It also means that **you don't have to turn the cube upside down** at some stage during your solve, which saves valuable seconds.

Second, **know the color scheme of your cube inside out**. Make sure that with the cross on the bottom, you know which colors are opposites of each other (look at directly opposite centers), and you know the order of the colors all the way around the cube. On my cube, I know that Red is opposite Orange, Blue is opposite Green, and if I have Red facing me, then Green is on the R-face, Blue is on the L-face, and Orange is on the B-face. This knowledge will allow you to concentrate on the other aspects of solving the cross. Learn your color scheme and practice it until it becomes second nature.

Relative Position and Edge "Flip"

Relative position is a concept that you must firmly fix in your mind before you can even hope to start seeing the shortest solutions to the cross for a given configuration.

If you think about it, it is not necessary to line up each edge with the same-colored center piece at a time, and then place them 1 at a time in the D-layer. This is a fine method if you are a beginner, or even intermediate, but if you want to start speedcubing seriously you must get out of this habit. This is where a good knowledge of your cube's color scheme is necessary. As long as you place, for example, the Red/White edge **opposite** the Orange/White edge, and the Blue/White edge **opposite** the Green/White edge, and you have made sure that the **colors are correct all the way round**, a **D** move will position the cross and fix all the pieces simultaneously every time. In other words, if you place the cross pieces incorrectly in the D-layer, but correctly *relative* to each other, you still get a solved cross (see Figure 5.1).

When you are pre-inspecting the cube, you will, of course, want to concentrate on the cross edges only, mentally blanking out the rest of the pieces altogether. Another useful thing to note about each cross edge as you inspect the cube is its "flip." But what is "flip"?

A CORRECTLY FLIPPED EDGE An edge that has a correct flip needs a **maximum of 1 move** to be inserted into the D-layer, in such a way

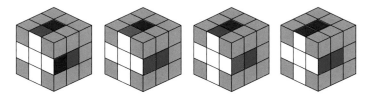

Figure 5.1 Using the concept of relative position, you can see that all of these crosses are solved; only D-turns are needed to fix all of the edges simultaneously.

Figure 5.2 The Orange edge is flipped correctly, only **F2** is required to place it into the D-layer.

so that it correctly forms a part of the cross (see Figure 5.2). It may already be sitting in the D-layer, in which case it does not need to be moved at all.

AN INCORRECTLY FLIPPED EDGE An edge that is incorrectly flipped will **always need 2 moves** to be inserted into the D-layer, to form part of the cross (see Figure 5.3). One move is required to correct its flip, and the other to insert it into the D-layer.

Edges that have an incorrect flip are the more difficult edges to solve, and you'll need to make special considerations when incorporating them

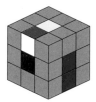

Figure 5.3 The Orange edge is incorrectly flipped; more than 1 move is needed to correct the flip and place it into the D-layer.

into your cross solution. These techniques are best shown and described in the examples at the end of the "Solving the Cross" section in "Example Cross Solutions."

The 3-Color Rule

Even when you have fully mastered the concept of relative position, it can be difficult to see at a glance whether or not certain cross pieces are in the correct positions relative to each other. A useful rule to help you decide is the 3-Color Rule, which is based on the colors of 2 edge pieces and the 2 center pieces they are connected to. Tables 5.2 and 5.3 demonstrate some of the possible scenarios for which you can apply this rule.

The 3-Color Rule breaks down if 1 or both of the connected edge/center pairs are the same color, or opposite colors. But in these cases, it is **much easier** to see whether or not the edges will place in the correct relative positions.

Putting It All Together

For each cube, you get only 1 chance at the cross. By learning these techniques, you can make the most of your pre-inspection time. It is important to realize how each technique helps the other, and how they overlap. However, the second component that helps you determine the shortest solution to each cross cannot be taught, for it is mastering the ability to see what happens to the cube as you apply 6 or 7 or 8 moves to it, in your head. In the following examples, I try to demonstrate as many tricks for solving or seeing ahead as I can, and I give a detailed description of the thought processes that go on in my head as I take 15 seconds to look at the cube. If you follow each example carefully, it should reinforce everything that I have said here and put it into a visual context. I hope you find these examples useful.

■ Table 5.2
3×3×3 Advanced Method—Solving the Cross: How to Apply the 3-Color Rule

Case	Explanation
	*If I move **R'**, will the cross edges be in the correct relative positions to one another?* The Green/White edge piece matches with the Red center, and the Red/White piece is connected to the Green center. White is the cross color, which can be ignored, meaning that we are looking at only **2 colors**–Green and Red. **2 colors = wrong**, which means that moving **R'** would not place the cross pieces in the correct relative positions.
	*If I move **F2**, will the cross edges be in the correct relative positions to one another?* A Blue/White edge is connected to the Red center, and a Red/White edge is connected to the Green center. Again we can ignore White, the cross color. The colors we are interested in are Blue, Red, and Green. **3 colors = correct**; therefore we can confidently say that after moving **F2**, the cross edges **will** be in the correct relative positions.
	*If I move **R'** followed by **F2**, will both cross edges be in the correct positions relative to one another?* At a glance, this question is not easily answered, unless you know the 3-Color Rule. Looking at the case, we see that the Blue/White edge is connected to the Red center, and the Orange/White edge is connected to the Green center. This time (again ignoring the cross color), we are looking at 4 colors–Blue, Red, Orange, and Green. **4 colors = wrong**, so by the 3-Color Rule we can see that **R'** followed by **F2** would not place these edges in the correct relative positions. However, moving **F2** followed by **L**, we move the Orange/White edge over to match the Blue center, eliminating the color Green and leaving us with 3 colors–Blue, Red, and Orange. This indicates that the cross edges are now in the correct relative positions.

■ Table 5.3
3×3×3 Advanced Method—Solving the Cross: How the 3-Color Rule Breaks Down

Case	Explanation
	In this case, we see 4 colors, but we also see (by knowing the color scheme) that both edge/center pairs are oppositely colored. So although we see 4 colors, it is easy to know that they are in the correct relative positions because a **D2** move would fix both pairs.
	Here we see only 2 colors, but since both edge/center pairs are matching colors, they are obviously in the correct positions.
	Here we see 3 colors. If we used the 3-Color Rule, we would think that these cross edges were in the correct positions. But **1 of the cross edges is the same color as the center** it is connected to, and **the other cross edge is the opposite color of the center** it is connected to. Although the rule suggests otherwise, we can easily see that these edges are **not** in the correct relative positions.

Example Cross Solutions

Example Scramble 1: R′ B2 U′ F2 L2 D′ U L′ F D2 R U2 B′ L R

We have 15 seconds for pre-inspection. What do we need to see?

- There are 3 correctly flipped cross edges (which can be placed in the D-layer in 1 move or less) and 1 incorrectly flipped cross edge (requiring 2 moves to place in the D-layer).
- The Orange/White piece at DF is in the D-layer, but it is matched up with an opposite-colored center (Red).
- The Green/White piece is matched up with the Green center and can be put in place with an **R** move.

- The Blue/White piece is in the U-layer and correctly flipped. We can move it to the D-layer with an **F2** move.
- The Red/White piece is in the U-layer and incorrectly flipped. We need to pay some attention to it.

Solution: First we take care of the incorrectly flipped edge. If we were to do **B** or **B′** to unflip the edge, we would move the Green/White edge out of place. We see that if we do **U′**, the Red/White edge is matched up with its opposite center (Green).

We can now do **R2** to place the Blue/White edge in the D-layer, then both Orange/White and Blue/White are in the correct relative positions, and it doesn't disturb the Green/White edge since we are turning the face with the Green center. Now we are free to move **L**, matching up the Red/White cross piece with the Red center and not disturbing any other cross edges.

We can now finish the cross in 3 more moves, but we must take care to apply them in the right order. First we move **D2** to fix the 2 edges in the D-layer and free up the slots for the remaining edges. Then we place the Green/White edge with **R′** (placing the Red/White edge with **F′** first would knock the Green edge out of place), and finally we finish the cross with **F′**.

U′ R2 L D2 R′ F′

Example Scramble 2: U B R2 B D B D′ U′ R′ D2 L2 U R B′ L′

We have 15 seconds for pre-inspection. What do we need to see?

- There are 2 correctly flipped edges, as well as 2 incorrectly flipped edges in the D-layer.
- The Blue/White edge is lined up with its opposite-colored center.
- The Green/White and Orange/White edges are incorrectly placed relative to each other; the Orange/White edge is matched with the Green center, and the Green/White edge with the Orange center: **2 colors = wrong**.

Solution: There are several possibilities; the 2 incorrectly flipped edges in the D-layer make this a particularly difficult case. **D′ R F** places the Orange/White and Green/White edges in the D-layer correctly. **B′** flips the Red/White edge correctly, and **L′** places it opposite the Orange/White edge, in the correct relative position. **D′** moves the cross around so that **R2** places the Blue/White edge in the correct relative position. Finally, **D2** solves all of the cross pieces.

D′ R F B′ L′ D′ R2 D2

This solution is long, at 8 moves, but with only 15 seconds of pre-inspection (which is all you get in a competition), it would be hard to find something shorter for this particularly difficult case. If you can manage to find a shorter solution, congratulations!

Don't be concerned if you are not able to solve the cross in 2 seconds or less straightaway. It takes most people many months to really master the cross to this extent, but with the knowledge of these techniques, you will be well on your way toward this mastery. As long as you are able to solve the cross, you are ready to learn the next step. The speed will come with practice.

First 2 Layers (F2L)

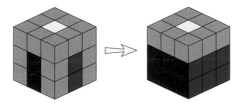

You saw in the beginner method that the F2L is solved in 2 distinct phases; first you solve the corners of the first layer, and then you solve the edges of the middle layer. The F2L in the CFOP system is a lot more advanced, however, since you solve both the first layer corners and middle layer edges simultaneously.

During this stage, you locate a "corner/edge pair" (simply a corner piece that belongs in the first layer, and the corresponding edge piece that belongs above it in the second layer), and you apply an algorithm to move these pieces into the correct "slot" (the name for the position on the cube where the solved pair resides). In most cases, you must perform this process 4 times, to solve each of the 4 corner/edge pairs that make up the F2L.

Tables 5.4 through 5.9 contain the complete set of 42 standard configurations of the first layer corner and corresponding middle layer edge, as well as algorithms to solve them into the FR position. I have subdivided them into categories based on the position and orientation of the corner piece, and these categories should be small enough so as to form manageable blocks of algorithms for you to learn in just 1 or 2 sessions. The letter denotes the face that the cross color on the corner piece is on, and a lowercase d indicates that the corner piece is in the bottom layer, as opposed to the top layer. The number corresponds to 1 of the 10 possible edge positions and orientations. You will notice for example, that the edge in Case #U2 is in the same position as in Case #R2, the only difference being that the white sticker is on the U face in #U2, and on the R face in #R2. There are many more ways to solve each case than the 1 algorithm I have given, but I have listed what I believe to be the fastest algorithms to solve in terms of both number of moves and ease of execution. They are the algorithms I currently use in speedsolving.

Many nonstandard configurations may crop up during your solves, and I give some advice on what to do when this happens in chapter 6. It is pretty much impossible to give clear-cut guidance on solving the F2L, for there are many hundreds of possible solutions for every case and many subtleties and nuances that you can learn only through experience. However, learning the tricks given in the tables is a good

■ **Table 5.4**
3×3×3 Advanced Method—First 2 Layers: Corner in U-Layer, Cross Color on U-Face

Case #U1
R U R' U' R U R' U' R U R'

Case #U2
R U' l U' R' U l'

Case #U3
(y') R' U2 R U R' U' R

Case #U4
U2 R2' U2 R' U' R U' R2'

Case #U5
d' L' U2' L U' L' U L

Case #U6
U2 R U R' U R U' R'

Case #U7
d2 (y) R' U' R U' R' U R

Case #U8
U R U2 R' U R U' R'

Case #U9
(y') U2 R2' U2 R U R' U R2

Case #U10
R U2 R' U' R U R'

starting point for any aspiring speedcuber, and once you master them, you will be well on your way to having a greater understanding of how best to solve the F2L.

Try to see how each algorithm works, and why it shuffles the corner and the edge around in the way it does; this will really help you learn them. Don't be put off by the number of cases; the algorithms are quite short and straightforward. Go through several solves slowly, look at what

■ Table 5.5
3×3×3 Advanced Method—First 2 Layers: Corner in
U-Layer, Cross Color on R-Face

Case #R1

d R' U R U2' R' U R

Case #R2

d R' U' R d' R U R'

Case #R3

d' L' U L

Case #R4

U R U' R' U' R U R' U' R U R'

Case #R5

d R' U' R U2' R' U R

Case #R6

U' R U R' U R U R'

Case #R7

d R' U2 R U2' R' U R

Case #R8

R U R'

Case #R9

R U' R' U2 (y') R' U' R

Case #R10

U' R U' R' U R U R'

cases appear on your cube, and use these tables to solve them. Slowly
build your knowledge and your speed, until you are able to efficiently
place each corner/edge pair together in the first 2 layers every time.

After solving the F2L, the powerful orientation and permutation steps
are all that stand in the way between you and the solved cube. We'll
learn these in the next sections.

■ Table 5.6
3×3×3 Advanced Method—First 2 Layers: Corner in U-Layer, Cross Color on F-Face

Case #F1

U' R U' R' U2 R U' R'

Case #F2

U' R U R' d R' U' R

Case #F3

d R' U R U' R' U' R

Case #F4

F' U F U2 R U R'

Case #F5

(y') R' U' R

Case #F6

U' R U2' R' U2 R U' R'

Case #F7

d R' U' R U' R' U' R

Case #F8

U' R U R' U2 R U' R'

Case #F9

d' L' U L U L' U' L U L' U' L

Case #F10

U R U' R'

■ Table 5.7
3×3×3 Advanced Method—First 2 Layers: Corner in Position, Oriented Correctly

Case #Dd1

Do nothing; the pair is solved!

Case #Dd2

R U' R' d R' U2 R U2' R' U R

Case #Dd3

U R U' R' d' L' U L

Case #Dd4

R U' R' U' R U' R' U R U R'

■ Table 5.8
3×3×3 Advanced Method—First 2 Layers: Corner in Position, Twisted Counterclockwise

 Case #Fd1

R U R' U' R U2 R' U' R U R'

 Case #Fd2

R U' R' d R' U' R U' R' U' R

 Case #Fd3

(y') R' U' R U R' U' R

 Case #Fd4

R U' R' U R U' R'

■ Table 5.9
3×3×3 Advanced Method—First 2 Layers: Corner in Position, Twisted Clockwise

Case #Rd1

R U2' R U R' U R U2' R2'

 Case #Rd2

R U' R' U2 (y') R' U' R U' R' U R

 Case #Rd3

(y') R' U R U' R' U R

 Case #Rd4

R U R' U' R U R'

Orient Last Layer (OLL)

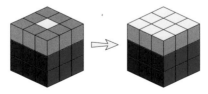

The Orient Last Layer step is the first of 2 steps needed to complete the last layer. During this step, you will correct the orientation (corner twist and edge flip) of every piece in the last layer, resulting in a solved up face, but not a solved up layer. This step has the most cases to learn, and many feel that mastering it represents the turning point from being a beginner to becoming an expert.

In Tables 5.10 to 5.23, you will find the 57 cases that you can encounter during the Orient Last Layer phase of the CFOP system, broken into bite-size chunks that should prove easier to learn. Cases are labelled in order of the number of U-face stickers showing on the U-face. It should be noted that due to my method of learning by categories, the case numbers appear to be random, an example being, #30 appears with cases #1-#7. The numbers are presented in this way on purpose,

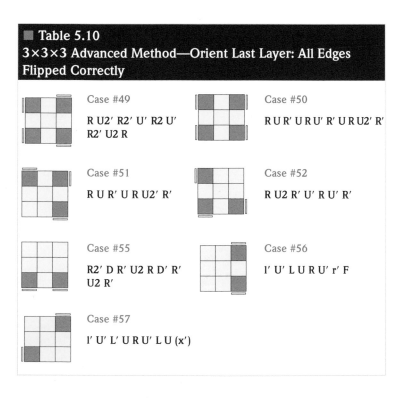

■ Table 5.10
3×3×3 Advanced Method—Orient Last Layer: All Edges Flipped Correctly

Case #49
R U2′ R2′ U′ R2 U′ R2′ U2 R

Case #50
R U R′ U R U′ R′ U R U2′ R′

Case #51
R U R′ U R U2′ R′

Case #52
R U2 R′ U′ R U′ R′

Case #55
R2′ D R′ U2 R D′ R′ U2 R′

Case #56
l′ U′ L U R U′ r′ F

Case #57
l′ U′ L′ U R U′ L U (x′)

■ Table 5.11
3×3×3 Advanced Method—Orient Last Layer: No Edges Flipped Correctly

 Case #01

R U (x′) U′ R U l′ R′
U′ l′ U l F′

 Case #02

F R U R′ U′ F′ f R U
R′ U′ f′

 Case #03

r′ R2 U R′ U r U2
r′ U R′ r

 Case #04

r′ R U′ r U2 r′ U′ R U′
R2′ r

 Case #05

r′ R U R U R′ U′ r R2′
F R F′

 Case #06

F R U R′ U (y′) R′ U2 R′
F R F′

 Case #07

R U R′ U R′ F R F′
U2 R′ F R F′

 Case #30

r′ R U R U R′ U′ r2 R2′
U R U′ r′

■ Table 5.12
3×3×3 Advanced Method—Orient Last Layer: T-Shapes

 Case #47

F R U R′ U′ F′

 Case #48

R U R′ U′ R′ F R F′

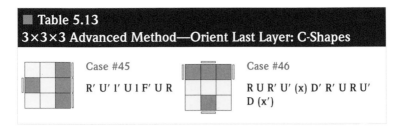

Table 5.13
3×3×3 Advanced Method—Orient Last Layer: C-Shapes

Case #45

R' U' l' U l F' U R

Case #46

R U R' U' (x) D' R' U R U' D (x')

Table 5.14
3×3×3 Advanced Method—Orient Last Layer: Squares

Case #20

r U2 R' U' R U' r'

Case #21

l' U2 L U L' U l

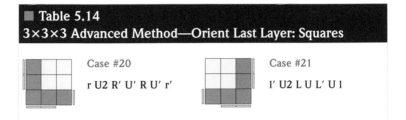

Table 5.15
3×3×3 Advanced Method—Orient Last Layer: Lightning Bolts

Case #22

r U R' U R U2 r'

Case #23

l' U' L U' L' U2' l

Case #24

r R2' U' R U' R' U2 R U' R r'

Case #25

r' R2 U R' U R U2 R' U R' r

Case #43

R' F R U R' U' F' U R

Case #44

L F' L' U' L U F U' L'

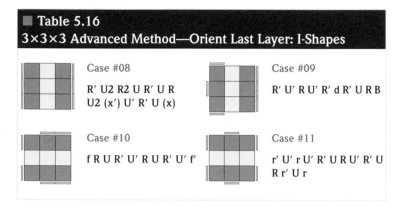

■ **Table 5.16**
3×3×3 Advanced Method—Orient Last Layer: I-Shapes

Case #08
R′ U2 R2 U R′ U R
U2 (x′) U′ R′ U (x)

Case #09
R′ U′ R U′ R′ d R′ U R B

Case #10
f R U R′ U′ R U R′ U′ f′

Case #11
r′ U′ r U′ R′ U R U′ R′ U
R r′ U r

and in my opinion, the best way to learn them is in the order in which they are presented here. It must be noted that there are many more ways to solve each case-different algorithms that achieve the same effect. However, I have tried many different algorithms in the past, and the ones below are the ones I have found to be the fastest, and the ones I currently use for speedcubing.

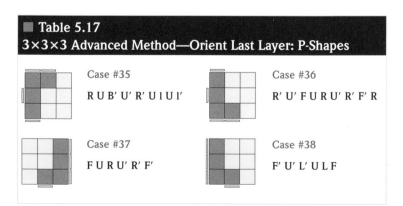

■ **Table 5.17**
3×3×3 Advanced Method—Orient Last Layer: P-Shapes

Case #35
R U B′ U′ R′ U l U l′

Case #36
R′ U′ F U R U′ R′ F′ R

Case #37
F U R U′ R′ F′

Case #38
F′ U′ L′ U L F

■ Table 5.18
3×3×3 Advanced Method—Orient Last Layer: L-Shapes

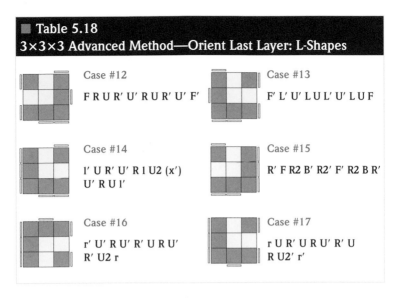

Case #12

F R U R' U' R U R' U' F'

Case #13

F' L' U' L U L' U' L U F

Case #14

l' U R' U' R l U2 (x')
U' R U l'

Case #15

R' F R2 B' R2' F' R2 B R'

Case #16

r' U' R U' R' U R U'
R' U2 r

Case #17

r U R' U R U' R' U
R U2' r'

■ Table 5.19
3×3×3 Advanced Method—Orient Last Layer: W-Shapes

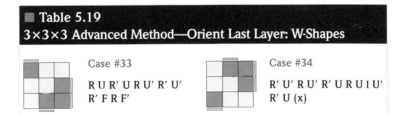

Case #33

R U R' U R U' R' U'
R' F R F'

Case #34

R' U' R U' R' U R U l U'
R' U (x)

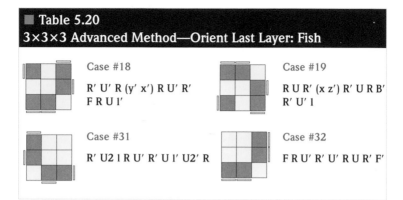

■ Table 5.20
3×3×3 Advanced Method—Orient Last Layer: Fish

Case #18

R' U' R (y' x') R U' R'
F R U 1'

Case #19

R U R' (x z') R' U R B'
R' U' 1

Case #31

R' U2 1 R U' R' U 1' U2' R

Case #32

F R U' R' U' R U R' F'

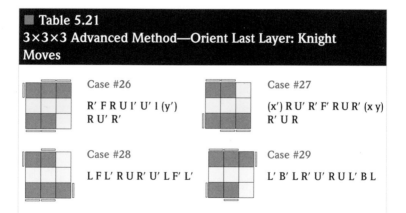

■ Table 5.21
3×3×3 Advanced Method—Orient Last Layer: Knight Moves

Case #26

R' F R U 1' U' 1 (y')
R U' R'

Case #27

(x') R U' R' F' R U R' (x y)
R' U R

Case #28

L F L' R U R' U' L F' L'

Case #29

L' B' L R' U' R U L' B L

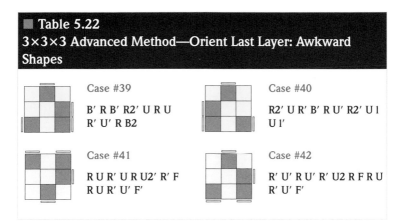

Table 5.22
3×3×3 Advanced Method—Orient Last Layer: Awkward Shapes

Case #39

B' R B' R2' U R U
R' U' R B2

Case #40

R2' U R' B' R U' R2' U 1
U 1'

Case #41

R U R' U R U2' R' F
R U R' U' F'

Case #42

R' U' R U' R' U2 R F R U
R' U' F'

To use the tables, identify which of the diagrams matches the pattern of stickers on your last layer. Then execute the corresponding algorithm.

Most cubers who learn CFOP leave the OLL until last. Don't try to learn it all in 1 go; it will take several months for you to get used to all of the cases. But even when you know only a small portion of the cases, when you are presented with one of them on the cube and you manage to solve it, it is very satisfying!

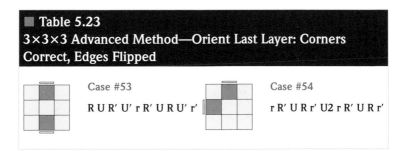

Table 5.23
3×3×3 Advanced Method—Orient Last Layer: Corners Correct, Edges Flipped

Case #53

R U R' U' r R' U R U' r'

Case #54

r R' U R r' U2 r R' U R r'

If you don't want to learn them all, you may find it useful to learn only the 7 cases in Table 5.10; combined with the permutation of the last layer (PLL) described in the next section, they form what is known as a 3-look last layer, a stepping stone between the beginner 4-look last layer and this expert CFOP 2-look last layer. When you get to the last layer, you first form a cross on the top, as in the beginner method, then you orient the last layer corners using one of those OLL algorithms, and finally you permute all last layer pieces with a PLL algorithm.

Permute Last Layer (PLL)

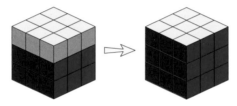

Permuting the last layer is the second of the 2 steps required to solve the last layer in this system. Here, you correct the positions (permutation) of each piece in the last layer, without changing their orientation. The end result is a completed last layer, and therefore a solved cube, provided you have kept the F2L intact. This stage has the longest sequences to learn, since you have the least freedom with which to move the pieces around. There are, however, only 21 cases, compared with the mammoth undertaking of the 57 OLL cases.

Tables 5.24 through 5.30 show algorithms to solve all 21 possible PLL cases. I have tried to organize the PLL algorithms into manageable, bite-size categories, which may help you structure your learning. Of course, feel free to learn them in any order you desire.

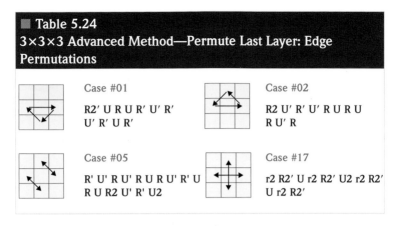

■ Table 5.24
3×3×3 Advanced Method—Permute Last Layer: Edge Permutations

Case #01

R2' U R U R' U' R'
U' R' U R'

Case #02

R2 U' R' U' R U R U
R U' R

Case #05

R' U' R U' R U R U' R' U
R U R2 U' R' U2

Case #17

r2 R2' U r2 R2' U2 r2 R2'
U r2 R2'

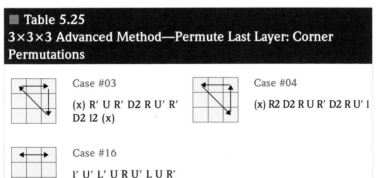

■ Table 5.25
3×3×3 Advanced Method—Permute Last Layer: Corner Permutations

Case #03

(x) R' U R' D2 R U' R'
D2 l2 (x)

Case #04

(x) R2 D2 R U R' D2 R U' l

Case #16

l' U' L' U R U' L U R'
U' L U R U' L' U (x')

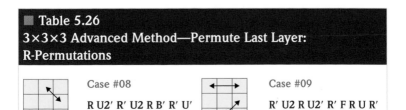

■ Table 5.26
3×3×3 Advanced Method—Permute Last Layer: R-Permutations

Case #08

R U2' R' U2 R B' R' U'
R U l U R2' F (x)

Case #09

R' U2 R U2' R' F R U R'
U' R' F' R2 U'

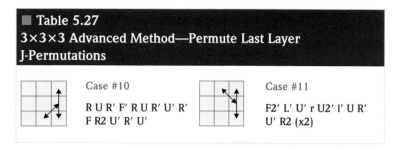

Table 5.27
3×3×3 Advanced Method—Permute Last Layer
J-Permutations

Case #10

R U R' F' R U R' U' R'
F R2 U' R' U'

Case #11

F2' L' U' r U2' l' U R'
U' R2 (x2)

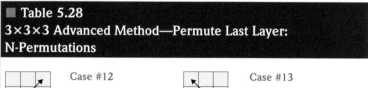

Table 5.28
3×3×3 Advanced Method—Permute Last Layer:
N-Permutations

Case #12

R U' L U2' R' U L' R
U' L U2' R' U L'

Case #13

L' U R' U2' L U L' L' R U
R' U2' L U' R

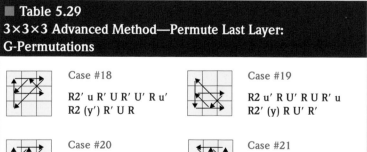

Table 5.29
3×3×3 Advanced Method—Permute Last Layer:
G-Permutations

Case #18

R2' u R' U R' U' R u'
R2 (y') R' U R

Case #19

R2 u' R U' R U R' u
R2' (y) R U' R'

Case #20

R U R' (y') R2 u' R U'
R' U R' u R2

Case #21

L' U' L (y') R2' u R' U
R U' R u' R2

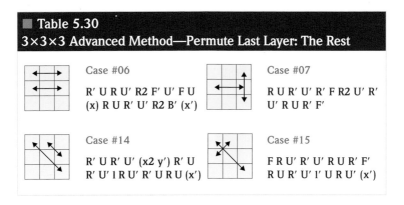

■ Table 5.30
3×3×3 Advanced Method—Permute Last Layer: The Rest

Case #06

R' U R U' R2 F' U' F U
(x) R U R' U' R2 B' (x')

Case #07

R U R' U' R' F R2 U' R'
U' R U R' F'

Case #14

R' U R' U' (x2 y') R' U
R' U' I R U' R' U R U (x')

Case #15

F R U' R' U' R U R' F'
R U R' U' I' U R U' (x')

To use the tables, try to identify the way in which you need to swap the pieces of your last layer. Try to line up as many pieces as you can before applying the PLL; this will help you recognize the cases at first. When you have found your case, execute the corresponding algorithm to permute the pieces.

Example Scrambles and Solutions Using the CFOP System
You have made it to the end of the CFOP system. Well done! It seems a daunting task at first—I know as I have been there myself—but with a lot of practice and the will to succeed in learning the method, you will be able to master this system and solve the cube in 20 seconds or less.

If you didn't understand some elements of the example solutions, especially relating to how the F2L algorithms appear to be executed differently from how they are presented in the F2L section, please read the advice in chapter 6 in the "First 2 Layers: Solving from All Angles" section, which may shed some light on your difficulties!

■ **Example Scramble 1 (start Red-F, Yellow-U, and Green-R to match picture): U2 L B2 F2 L′ D2 L2 D′ B′ R′ B F2 R′ B2 F2 D2 U L2 R U′ F D′ U F2 L2**

Cross:

- **B2 D F′ B2 D2**

First 2 Layers:

- **U2 y′ R U R′ d R′ U′ R**—First pair
- **U R U′ R B′ R′ B R′**—Second pair
- **U2 L′ U L U L′ U′ L**—Third pair
- **y2 U′ R U2 R′ U′ R U R′**—Fourth pair

Orient Last Layer:

- **U′ R′ U′ R U′ R′ U2 R F R U R′ U′ F′**—One of the "awkward shapes"

Permute Last Layer:

- **F2′ L′ U′ r U2′ l′ U R′ U′ R2 D2**—An "upside-down" J-permutation

■ **Example Scramble 2:** L B2 F D′ B F′ L2 B2 F2 L B′ F L2 B′ F′ R D′ U′ F U′ F D2 B′ F2 U′

Cross:

▪ L′ B′ U′ R′ F D B′ D

First 2 Layers:

▪ d R′ U′ R U′ R′ U R
▪ d L′ U L
▪ U R′ U2 R U′ R′ U R
▪ y′ R′ U R U′ R′ U′ R

Orient Last Layer:

▪ y2 x′ R U′ R′ F′ R U R′ x y R′ U R—A "knight move" OLL case

Permute Last Layer:

▪ y2 x R2 D2 R U R′ D2 R U′ l—A 3-corner cycle permutation

6

Expert 3×3×3 Speedcubing Techniques

This chapter gives you insight into advanced techniques that will allow you to expand on your basic knowledge of the CFOP system and refine some aspects of your solving. Most of the sections are aimed at improving your speed in the First 2 Layers (F2L) stage, which is where most people gain a lot more time. The reason for this is simple: whereas the Orient Last Layer (OLL) and Permute Last Layer (PLL) stages are brute-force approaches—it's just a case of how fast you can recognize each case and perform each algorithm—the F2L is more subtle and allows you to express yourself more freely. After achieving the cross, you can take several different paths through the F2L, and it is a daunting task to rapidly select the fastest one. By applying some of the following tips, you will gain a better understanding of how the pros manage this.

Read through the sections in order, because each one builds upon knowledge gained in the previous, and by the end of the chapter you will have acquired as much knowledge as the world's elite cubers. Then it's just a matter of getting a lot of cubing experience!

FINGER TRICKS

One of the easiest ways to quickly become faster is to incorporate finger tricks into your solutions. Finger tricks are sequences of moves that you can perform in 1 fluid hand movement.

For example, the move sequence **(R′ U R′)** is a finger trick. Begin by holding the R-layer so that your thumb is on the UF sticker, your index finger is on the DBR sticker, and your remaining fingers help to grip the R-layer. Turn your hand to make the move **R′**. Now your index finger is on the BUR sticker, and you can use this to push the U-layer to make a **U** move. Finally, continue the hand movement to make the final **R′**. You can perform these 3 moves in the time it takes to execute **R2**.

You can use your index finger and thumb to perform a variety of finger tricks, such as **(R U R′), (R U′ R), (R U′ R′), (R′ F), (R B′),** and many more. Play around with your cube and experiment to find finger tricks that work for you. By incorporating these into your solves, you can rapidly decrease your solving times, but the amount of time you gain will depend a lot on how stable and easy to turn your cube is.

FIRST 2 LAYERS: PAIR UP AND INSERT

Learning the concepts of "pair up" and "insert" is the first and perhaps greatest step on the road to full F2L mastery. Most algorithms that you use for the F2L (including the ones in this book) follow these concepts, with only a few minor exceptions. It is very important, if you want to become fast, that you understand how each F2L algorithm first "pairs up" the corner and edge, and then "inserts" them into the correct position, rather than just blindly applying the algorithm to solve the corner/edge pair. Only when you fully understand this will you be able to take your cubing to a higher level.

Pairing Up and Inserting

F2L algorithms shuffle the corner and edge around in such a way that the pieces can be paired up in 2 distinct ways: a "connected pair" or a "separated pair," as shown in Table 6.1.

The **most** important thing to realize is that nearly every F2L algorithm you come across sets up 1 of these situations, and then you add a couple of moves to the end to insert the pair and maybe to restore other pairs that broke up during the "pair-up" process. That's the way in which they work. Table 6.2 shows some examples.

When you have some spare time, examine some of your F2L algorithms and see how they work in terms of the pair-up and insert process. You will gain a greater understanding of how each algorithm works, and this new knowledge will help you put into practice the techniques described in later sections.

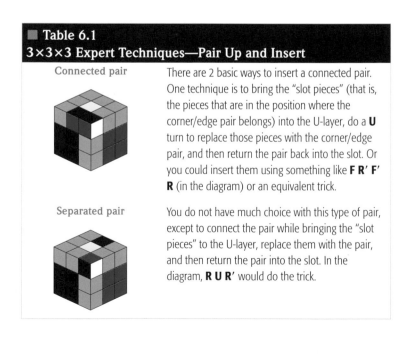

■ Table 6.1	
3×3×3 Expert Techniques—Pair Up and Insert	
Connected pair	There are 2 basic ways to insert a connected pair. One technique is to bring the "slot pieces" (that is, the pieces that are in the position where the corner/edge pair belongs) into the U-layer, do a **U** turn to replace those pieces with the corner/edge pair, and then return the pair back into the slot. Or you could insert them using something like **F R' F' R** (in the diagram) or an equivalent trick.
Separated pair	You do not have much choice with this type of pair, except to connect the pair while bringing the "slot pieces" to the U-layer, replace them with the pair, and then return the pair into the slot. In the diagram, **R U R'** would do the trick.

Table 6.2
3×3×3 Expert Techniques—Pair Up and Insert Examples

Case	Explanation
Do F' U' F U2 F' U F U' to set up. 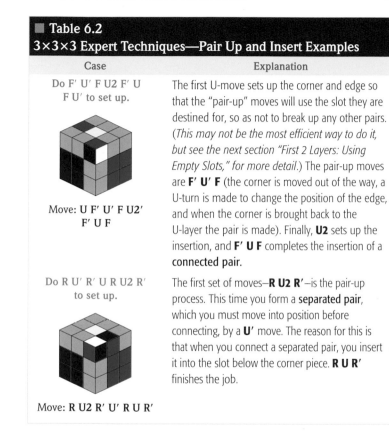 Move: U F' U' F U2' F' U F	The first U-move sets up the corner and edge so that the "pair-up" moves will use the slot they are destined for, so as not to break up any other pairs. *(This may not be the most efficient way to do it, but see the next section "First 2 Layers: Using Empty Slots," for more detail.)* The pair-up moves are **F' U' F** (the corner is moved out of the way, a U-turn is made to change the position of the edge, and when the corner is brought back to the U-layer the pair is made). Finally, **U2** sets up the insertion, and **F' U F** completes the insertion of a **connected pair**.
Do R U' R' U R U2 R' to set up.	The first set of moves—**R U2 R'**—is the pair-up process. This time you form a **separated pair**, which you must move into position before connecting, by a **U'** move. The reason for this is that when you connect a separated pair, you insert it into the slot below the corner piece. **R U R'** finishes the job.

Move: **R U2 R' U' R U R'**

FIRST 2 LAYERS: USING EMPTY SLOTS

"Empty slots" are F2L slots that have not yet been solved. It is really useful to keep track of where your empty slots are, because you can use them to your advantage when trying to reduce the number of moves, changes of grip, and rotations while you execute a speed solution. To become fast and fluent at the F2L, you must keep all these moves to a minimum.

You get the chance to use empty slots during the pair-up stage of solving the current F2L pair (see Table 6.2 for a description of "pair-up" and "insert"). The standard algorithms presented in Tables 5.4–5.9 are designed to disturb only the slot that you will eventually solve the pair into, which means you can use them at any stage in the F2L. But this isn't usually the most efficient way, since using empty slots can:

- Make a "standard" cube rotation or setup move unnecessary
- Reduce the number of moves needed to solve the current pair
- Break up a difficult pair trapped in the F2L

Tables 6.3 through 6.5 show some examples of scenarios in which you could use empty slots to achieve all of these.

I hope these examples have helped you to better understand how to use empty slots to your advantage. I have shown you the advantages you can gain and how they will save you time, but I have by no means shown you how to use empty slots for every possible F2L case. There is no substitute for lots of practice using empty slots. You must investigate for yourself how each of your F2L moves disturbs the other slots and what time advantages you can gain from your newfound knowledge. Once you master the use of empty slots, you will see a definite decrease in your times and a greater fluidity and rhythm in your solving. When you couple this technique with the ability to solve pieces from all angles, as discussed in the next section, you will begin to see how the world's best can put together the entire F2L in under 10 seconds.

■ Table 6.3
3×3×3 Expert Techniques—Empty Slots Examples:
Making a Cube Rotation or Setup Move Unnecessary

Do L' U L U R U R' on a solved cube to set up.

Move: U y' R U' R'
U2 y L' U' L

The standard way to solve it

The standard algorithm for this case breaks up the slot beneath the corner piece. So the first **U** is to set up the correct position. From this position it is quite awkward to execute the pair-up moves, so you might decide to rotate (**y'**) before executing **R U' R' U2**. It is again awkward from here to execute the insertion moves, so you might decide to rotate back again (**y**) before executing **L' U' L**. However you perform the move, you will have to rotate or change your grip to execute the move, which may consume half a second.

Move: R U' R' U' L' U' L

Solving using an empty slot

With experience, you will recognize the standard procedure to break up or pair up a corner/edge pair in this configuration. It always disturbs the slot beneath the corner piece, and if this slot is empty, you can make use of it.

In this case, the moves **R U' R'** pair up the corner/edge pair and disturb the FR slot (beneath the corner piece). But because this slot is empty, you don't care if you disturb it! That is the crucial thing when using empty slots. You are now free to do **U'** to set up the insertion, and finally **L' U' L** to insert. You haven't rotated, and because of that you haven't lost any rhythm or momentum, or time.

With experience you will find that you can solve this particular F2L case without rotating if the empty slot you are using is an adjacent slot to the 1 you

continued on next page

continued from previous page

are solving it into. If you are solving it using a diagonally opposite empty slot, you will still have to rotate.

■ Table 6.4
3×3×3 Expert Techniques—Empty Slots Examples: Reducing the Number of Moves Needed to Solve the Current Pair

Do R U' R2 U2 R on a solved cube to set up.

Move: R' U2 R2' U
R2' U R

The standard way to solve it

The pair-up move for this case disturbs the slot that is "behind" the corner piece. This is because the pair-up procedure hides the corner piece in the bottom layer (which in turns brings up the slot pieces behind the corner) while you move the edge round to other side. Bringing the corner back up connects the pair. So pairing up is **R' U2 R2'**, and you have disturbed the slot behind the corner (the BR slot). The rest of the moves insert the pair and finally restore the BR pair that you initially disturbed, by **U R2' U R**.

Move: R' U2 R2' U R'

Solving using an empty slot

If the BR slot is empty, then you don't care if you disturb it. This means you don't have to waste moves restoring it, and you can finish the move by just inserting the pair. **R' U2 R2'** is the pair-up; **U R'** is the insert.

You have saved 2 moves compared with the standard way of solving. If you are cubing at 2 to 3 moves per second, you have slashed from 0.66 to 1 second off your time.

■ Table 6.5
3×3×3 Expert Techniques—Empty Slots Examples:
Breaking Up a Difficult Pair Trapped in the F2L

Do R U' R2 U' R F' U' F U B' R' U' R U B U2 B U2' B' U
on a solved cube to set up.

Move: **U2 y R U R'**
U R U' R'

The standard way to solve it

A good trick for cases where the corner piece has the cross color on top, and the edge is separated from the corner in the U-layer, is to line up the edge color around the side with its center color (**U2 y**, Orange in the diagram), then move the edge into the middle layer, while at the same time bringing up the slot pieces (**R**) from the slot that you intend to solve the pieces into. Finally, you can pair up the corner with the edge by making **U** moves (**U**), and insert as usual (**R' U R U' R'**). This is the basis of the standard way, and it is fine to do in this case. But the situation of the other pair (the FR pair) might mean that you choose to do something different.

Solving using an empty slot

Move: **U' R U R' y R U' R'**

The situation of the FR pair is awkward to solve, and the solution can be long and slow. You might simply release the pair and then solve the resulting F2L case (for example, **R U' R'**), or if you were smart, you would use it as an empty slot, which would disturb the pair and set up a new case while at the same time place the other pair (BR pair). In this case, **U' R U R'** makes the pair, utilizing the FR slot as an empty slot. **y R U' R'** is the simple insertion.

  Although you still had to rotate, you have set up a much simpler case for the final pair compared with what you had before. It can take quite a bit of

continued on next page

continued from previous page

experience to see which way you have to move
the edge initially to make the pair. If you had tried
F′ U2 F, you would have found that the edge ends
up connected to the corner, but flipped incorrectly.

As an afterthought, you could solve the final
pair nicely without having to rotate using the
nonstandard F2L algorithm **r′ R U′ R′ F R U R′ r**.

FIRST 2 LAYERS: SOLVING FROM ALL ANGLES

It is a myth that to be able to solve pairs into all 4 possible F2L slots you
must learn 4 sets of F2L algorithms; this is just not the case. You can
expand what you know about pair up and insert and empty slots to all
4 F2L slots; in this section you will learn how to interpret the situation
and use tricks to be able to solve with minimal rotation and maximum
fluidity.

As discussed before, you can solve just about every F2L situation
using a "pair up and insert" algorithm. To solve pairs into different slot
positions (different angles), you must interpret your pair-up maneuver
in a slightly different way from how you may have been doing up to now.

Instead of remembering a strict set of moves that will pair up the
corner and edge into either a separated or connected pair—for example,
R′ U R—you must imagine the movement that your hands have to do
to pair up the pieces, which I like to call a "trick." This is an important
part of making the transition from remembering and recalling the
algorithms in your brain to moving the muscles in your hands to perform
the same feat—muscle memory. By seeing it this way, when you have
to solve a pair into a slot other than **FR**, it will be much easier to imagine
how you might move your hands to pair up the pieces, rather than trying
to transform notation in your head to achieve the same result. Eventually,
after much practice, you will just "know" what to do.

■ Table 6.6
3×3×3 Expert Techniques—Solving from All Angles:
The Pair-Up Trick for Case #F3

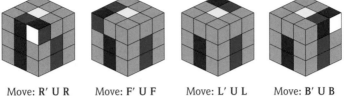

| Move: **R′ U R** | Move: **F′ U F** | Move: **L′ U L** | Move: **B′ U B** |

Imagine you knew only the pair-up trick for the situation in the first cube. That is, after all, the position given in most sets of F2L algorithms, including the tables in this book, and is therefore the position that most people learn. You know that to pair them up, you must do **R′ U R**. But if you were going at top speed and you encountered 1 of the cases in the other 3 cubes, would you realize that they are the same case, and could you transform that move into **F′ U F, L′ U L**, or **B′ U B** in a split second?

What you really need to know is the trick in terms of how the pieces move relative to each other. In this case, when I learned it, I remembered this procedure:

- Move the layer that the corner is on so that the cross color goes onto the D-face.
- Move the edge away from the corner by 1 quarter turn.
- Bring the corner back into the U-layer.

I also know that this pair-up trick disturbs the slot behind the corner. Armed with this information, you can see how it is easy to do the same thing at all 4 angles! No matter which angle you view the case from, the procedure will always be the same. Knowing the trick in terms of how the pieces move (that is, what your hands have to do) can help you solve the pair at all angles, because once you have paired them up, you can easily insert the pieces into any slot. No matter which slot they belong to, no matter how they are angled in the U-layer, if they correspond to case #F3, you can use this procedure to pair up the pieces.

The pair-up stage is all you really need to concentrate on in this tutorial, shown in Tables 6.6 and 6.7, because once you have paired up, you can easily see the insertion trick, and with practice this will become natural to you. Once you have the hang of this, you can start putting it together with what you know about empty slots to choose the most efficient way to solve each pair into any F2L slot you need.

Even with just these 2 examples, you should be able to see the potential of this technique for solving pieces into any slot. This technique works with almost all F2L algorithms, and it's up to you to investigate the tricks that work for the various cases and which slot (seconds) the trick affects. This, coupled with the usual copious amount of practice, should allow you to become much more fluid when solving the F2L.

■ **Table 6.7**
3×3×3 Expert Techniques—Solving from All Angles:
The Pair-Up Trick for Case #R5

Move: **R′ U′ R**   Move: **F′ U′ F**   Move: **L′ U′ L**   Move: **B′ U′ B**

This time, the procedure is:

- Move the corner down to the D-layer, so that the cross color stays on the same face.
- Move the edge toward the corner 1 quarter turn.
- Bring the corner back into the U-layer.

Again, this pair-up trick disturbs the slot behind the corner. So if the slot behind the corner is empty, then you can pair up the pieces using these tricks! That's all there is to it.

Remember to look out for empty slots; if you have a choice of empty slots, you can work out which 1 lets you solve the pieces without rotation. Do this slowly at first; eventually you will build back up to top speed.

FIRST 2 LAYERS: TRAPPED PIECES

Pieces trapped in the first 2 layers are notoriously awkward to solve. The algorithms to solve "standard" cases, where pieces are trapped in the correct slot but wrongly oriented, are rather long-winded, and pieces trapped in a wrong slot can be even more troublesome. Solving the F2L would be much easier without these situations.

There are 3 main ways to deal with these cases:

- **Know an algorithm to solve the case**. This is fine for the standard cases where the pieces are trapped in the correct slot. To know algorithms for all nonstandard cases is a lot to ask, but it's doable. A nonstandard case with a simple yet nonintuitive solution is known as a shortcut, and some experienced cubers use a lot of shortcuts in their speedsolving. Personally, I don't believe this is the most effective way of dealing with these cases, although for some special cases I also use shortcuts.
- **Use a simple trick to release the pieces and place them into the U-layer, and then solve the resulting case**. This is the simplest way to deal with these cases but probably not the most efficient. There are occasions in which the case you are left with is still difficult and long-winded to solve, and you could add unnecessary moves to your solution in the process. However, sometimes there is nothing better to do.
- **Treat the slot containing the pieces as an empty slot, so they are released into the U-layer when solving another pair**. This is the smartest way to release a trapped pair, but it also requires the most knowledge and experience in solving using empty slots.

Tables 6.8 through 6.10 give examples of each technique. Following these with a real cube will give you better insight into each situation.

■ **Table 6.8**
**3×3×3 Expert Techniques—Pieces Trapped in the F2L:
Solving the Case Using a Standard Algorithm or a Shortcut**

Do R U' R' F' L' U2 L F to set up.

This case is a standard case (#Fd2) listed in the set of 41 F2L cases in chapter 5. You can find more examples of cases like this in the Fd and Rd categories.

Move: **R U' R' d R' U' R
U' R' U' R**

Do R' U R F R' F' R to set up.

This is an example of a nonstandard case, which you won't find listed in any sets of F2L algorithms. Unless you know this shortcut, it can be quite a difficult case to solve, and certainly not achievable in 7 moves.

Move: **R' F R F' R' U' R**

■ Table 6.9
3×3×3 Expert Techniques—Pieces Trapped in the F2L: Displacing the Trapped Pair Using a Simple Trick

Do R U' R' U B U' B' U2 to set up.

Move: **R' U' R**

In this situation, the FR edge is trapped in the BR slot. The DFR corner is in the U-layer, at UBR. The trick **R' U' R** displaces the trapped edge and the result is a standard case that you can solve with a standard algorithm.

You must be careful when using this technique. It's not a good idea to just blindly apply a trick–for example, if instead of the move described, you actually applied **R' U R** to release the edge. This works, but now you have trapped the corner in a wrong slot and are back to where you started! You have to keep an eye out for this.

■ Table 6.10
3×3×3 Expert Techniques—Pieces Trapped in the F2L: Treating the Slot Containing Trapped Pieces as an Empty Slot

Do R U' R' F' L' U2 L F R' U' R U2 R' U R to set up.

Move: **d R' U' R d L' U L**

The BR pair is a standard case; normally you would use **R' U' R** to pair up and **U2 R' U R** to insert. However, you can see that this leaves an awkward pair in the FR slot. You could use this as an empty slot when pairing up the BR pair. The pair-up moves disturb the BR slot, so first do **d** to move the FR slot into the BR position. Then do the pair-up, which now disturbs the awkward pair, **R' U' R**. Finish off with **d L' U L**, and you are left with a much easier pair to solve last. You have added only 1 extra move to the solution, and you save time by having an easier pair to solve at the end.

Being able to confidently deal with awkward cases is a big part of speedcubing. Solve your F2L slowly at first and look for occasions where you can apply these techniques. Practice them until they become natural to you. Eventually you will find that you don't have to make a decision each time; you will just "know" the best way to deal with each case.

INFLUENCING THE LAST LAYER DURING THE FIRST 2 LAYERS

To improve solution times, some speedcubers have wondered if they need a faster last layer strategy (LL). Fridrich's OLL and PLL stages are hard to beat in this respect; probably the only way that could be faster theoretically is to learn all the algorithms required to solve the last layer in 1 step. In practice, though, even this strategy would struggle against the powerful OLL + PLL, because the cases would be difficult and time-consuming to recognize, and it would take a superhuman effort to memorize all of the algorithms in the first place. Some current work has been devoted, therefore, to preparing the last layer during the F2L stage, to reduce the number of possible last layer cases and make different strategies possible. Most of the focus has been on manipulating the LL edges while solving the F2L. One method is to orient all edges at the beginning of the solution, before making the cross. A more common strategy is to orient the LL edges and solve the final F2L pair simultaneously. In this section, I show you two methods that let you prepare the last layer in this way, along with possible continuations once you have achieved this.

Vandenbergh-Harris F2L

The Vandenbergh-Harris F2L makes use of the fact, which I keep reiterating, that most F2L algorithms have distinct pair-up and insert phases. It was invented by Lars Vandenbergh of Belgium and myself, Dan Harris of the United Kingdom, as a clever technique for influencing the LL during the final step of the F2L. Known as the VHF2L, the strategy is to first pair up the final corner/edge pair into either a separated or connected pair. The final corner/edge pair is then inserted using a special insertion trick, which solves the pair and simultaneously orients all LL edges. There are only 32 cases to learn—16 where you have a connected pair and 16 where you have a separated pair—and they are all straightforward to apply. Table 6.11 gives you an example.

Tables 6.12 and 6.13 contain the complete set of VHF2L insertion tricks. To use them, when you arrive at the final pair of the F2L, pair up the corner and edge in the usual way, and then identify which of the following 32 cases you are left with. Once you have identified it, use the corresponding algorithm to solve it and orient all LL edges. Be careful—

■ Table 6.11
3×3×3 Expert Techniques—VHF2L Examples:
Influencing the LL Edges Using the VHF2L

Do R U′ R′ F′ U2 F U′ R′ F R F′ U′ on a solved cube to set up.

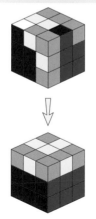

The standard way to solve

Normally you would solve this case with **R U2 R′ U R U′ R′**. This solves the F2L and leaves 2 edges incorrectly oriented.

Move: **R U2 R′ U R U′ R′**

continued on next page

continued from previous page

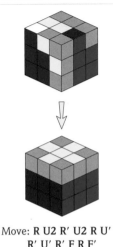

Solving using VHF2L

The beginning of the algorithm is exactly the same, since the first few moves complete the pair-up phase, which is integral to VHF2L. **R U2 R'** forms a connected pair. The insertion trick for the resulting case is then **U2 R U' R' U' R' F R F'**, which solves the F2L **and** correctly orients all LL edges. Although the algorithm is now substantially longer, it is fairly intuitive, and you can execute it fast with lots of quick finger triggers.

Move: **R U2 R' U2 R U'**
R' U' R' F R F'

if you are unlucky, you will have a case for which your algorithm isn't a simple pair up and insert, and in these cases it is very awkward to do anything about it. That is where learning a specialized algorithm has a big advantage.

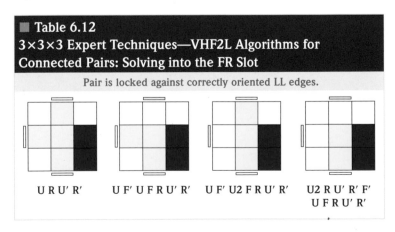

■ Table 6.12
3×3×3 Expert Techniques—VHF2L Algorithms for Connected Pairs: Solving into the FR Slot

Pair is locked against correctly oriented LL edges.

U R U' R'	U F' U F R U' R'	U F' U2 F R U' R'	U2 R U' R' F' U F R U' R'

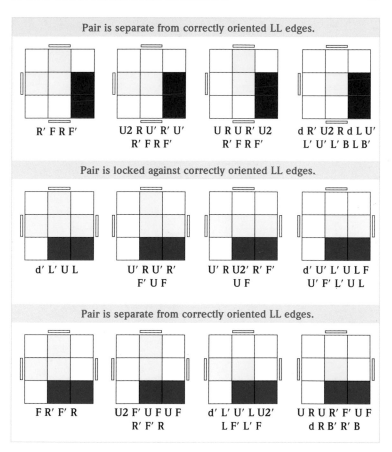

Pair is separate from correctly oriented LL edges.

R' F R F'

U2 R U' R' U'
R' F R F'

U R U R' U2
R' F R F'

d R' U2 R d L U'
L' U' L' B L B'

Pair is locked against correctly oriented LL edges.

d' L' U L

U' R U' R'
F' U F

U' R U2' R' F'
U F

d' U' L' U L F
U' F' L' U L

Pair is separate from correctly oriented LL edges.

F R' F' R

U2 F' U F U F
R' F' R

d' L' U' L U2'
L F' L' F

U R U R' F' U F
d R B' R' B

■ Table 6.13
3×3×3 Expert Techniques—VHF2L Algorithms for
Separated Pairs: Solving into the FR Slot

R U R'

R U' R' U' R U
R' U2 R' F R F'

R U' R' U2 R'
F R F'

R U' R' U' F'
U2 F R U' R'

R U2' R' U'
R' F R F'

R U2' R' F' U F
R U' R'

R U' R' U' F' U
F R U' R'

R U' R' F' U F U2 R
U R' U2 R' F R F'

F' U' F

F' U' F2 U R
U' R' F'

F' U F U2 F
R' F' R

F' U F U R
U2' R' F' U F

F' U2 F U F
R' F' R

F' U2 L' U L F

F' U2 F R U2'
R' F' U F

F D B' R' B D'
F2 U' F

You should approach these algorithms in the same way that you approach the normal F2L algorithms. Understand how they change the edges, and by doing so you can apply other things you now know, such as solving from all angles.

In general, fewer correctly oriented LL edges means working harder to achieve correct orientation, and therefore the algorithms are longer. The algorithms for the cases where no edges are correctly oriented to start with are pretty awful, and you wouldn't really gain any time advantage if you used this method to solve them. Once you become familiar with the VHF2L method, it might be a good idea to see if you can change the edges when solving the third pair. If you can always end up with 2 LL edges flipped correctly when reaching the fourth pair, you will not have so much work to do with the fourth pair. Table 6.14 demonstrates this nicely. Don't worry if it seems incomprehensible at first; with practice, it will begin to make more sense.

■ Table 6.14
3×3×3 Expert Techniques—VHF2L Examples: Flipping Edges During the Third Pair

Do R U R' U R U2 R' F R U R' U' F' R U R' U' R U' R' U L F' L' F2 U F' U' to set up.

Move: **d R U' R' U2 F' U F U2 R U' R' U' R' U' R U' R'** **U R**

You're at the third pair of the F2L, and it's not looking good. If you solve the third pair using a standard algorithm, you will probably end up with an awkward VHF2L case to solve. So you might decide to try and change things for the better during the third pair.

Going for the FL pair while changing the edges

Do a standard pair-up move, **d R U' R'**, and a connected pair is now in the top layer. Now, instead

continued on next page

continued from previous page

of inserting this pair in the normal way (that is, **U R U′ R′** or **R′ F R F′**), you can be a bit more clever in how you approach it. **U2** moves the pair out of the way, ready for the next piece of the puzzle, **F′ U F**. This trick inserts another correctly oriented LL edge into the last layer, without disturbing the connected pair. By doing the extra work here, you make it much easier to finish with 4 correctly oriented LL edges after solving the whole F2L.

Insert the third pair

With a bit of practice, you will be able to spot that the correct insertion here is **U2 R U′ R′**. This brings 3 correctly oriented LL edges to the U-layer, and by recognizing that you can solve the fourth pair using a 2-generator algorithm, you can deduce that all edges are correctly oriented. If you use a 2-generator algorithm (an algorithm that uses only 2 sides), the edge orientation will not change, and you can guarantee 4 correctly flipped edges after solving the fourth pair.

Solve the fourth pair using 2-gen

U′ sets up the case using our little edge color trick, and **R′ U′ R U′ R′ U R** is the 2-gen algorithm you need to solve the pair. *Voila*—4 correctly flipped LL edges with minimal effort!

As an aside, if you were very sharp, you might have spotted that after **d R U′ R′ U2 F′ U F** it is possible to insert the BR pair without undoing the connected FR pair and without disturbing the edge orientation. You therefore would have a slightly shorter solution, while still orienting all 4 LL edges: **U R′ U′ R U R U′ R′**. But these types of shortcuts are easy to miss, and it takes a lot of experience to be able to spot them at top speed.

Remember:

- Every algorithm of the "pair up and insert" variety can be modified to include these VHF2L tricks.
- You have the ability to choose the way you insert the pieces; the trick you choose will determine the final orientation of the LL edges.
- If the situation is looking tough by the time you get to the third pair, remember that you have the option to orient at least 2 edges while solving the third pair.
- Know that if you have 3 LL edges correctly oriented in the U-layer by the time you get to the fourth pair, and you get a fourth pair case that can be solved using a 2-gen algorithm, all the edges are correctly oriented.
- 2-generator algorithms do not disturb edge orientation.

Practice solving as many cubes as you can and go through the transition stage from the final couple of F2L pairs to the LL very slowly, trying each time to flip edges. The more you practice, the more you will discover about the technique. You will begin to see naturally which insertions to use and how to smartly use the edge "overlap," and soon you won't need to know the tricks as set moves. Then you can start applying the tricks at all angles.

As I have mentioned before, there are cases for which this particular strategy doesn't work. The algorithms for these cases would not have separate pair-up and insert stages, but they would solve the pieces more directly. Another, more brute-force approach to influencing the LL is the ZBF2L, described in the next section.

Zborowski-Bruchem F2L

Invented independently by Ron van Bruchem of The Netherlands and Zbigniew Zborowski of Poland, the ZB system is a brute-force approach to solving the final stages of the cube. For the ZBF2L part, the idea is the same as the VHF2L: solve the final pair and orient the LL edges correctly. However, to achieve this requires knowing a specific algorithm for every combination of standard F2L cases and LL edge orientations, resulting in a mammoth 306 cases to learn. It is beyond the scope of this book to list all of these cases and algorithms, but in Tables 6.15 through 6.17 I give some examples of how you might put ZBF2L into practice during your solves.

■ Table 6.15
3×3×3 Expert Techniques—ZBF2L Examples: Same F2L Case, Different Algorithms

Do R U' R' d U R' U' R y to set up.

Move: **y' R' U R U' d' R U R'**

The standard "pair up and insert" trick is the algorithm that solves this case. The correct edges on the LL are in a "backward L shape," and this algorithm flips the UR and FR edges so that when they are placed in the U-layer, they are oriented correctly. When the edges are in this pattern for this case, the algorithm **y' R' U R U' d' R U R'** will always solve the pair and orient all the edges.

Do l L' U L F L' U' L l' to set up.

Move: l **L' U L F' L' U' L l'**

This second example has the same F2L case as the first example, but a different LL edge situation. This time, the correct edge pieces on the LL form a horizontal line. Applying the algorithm **l L' U L F' L' U' L l'** solves this particular case and orients all the LL edges at the same time. Applying the algorithm from the first example would solve the F2L case but leave 2 LL edges flipped incorrectly, so you must choose this particular algorithm if you want to orient all 4 LL edges correctly.

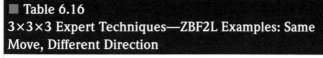

■ Table 6.16
3×3×3 Expert Techniques—ZBF2L Examples: Same Move, Different Direction

Do R B′ R B R′ U R′ to set up.

Move: **R U′ R B′ R′ B R′**

Do y′ R′ F R′ F′ R U′ R y to set up.

Move: **y′ R′ U R′ F R F′ R**

This example was the first example I ever learned, and it is a neat demonstration of how an easy-to-make split-second choice makes all the difference. The algorithm to solve this pair is very nice and can be executed from many different directions. When you have 3 LL edges correctly flipped in the U-layer, then the fourth will also be in the U-layer, flipped incorrectly. To orient all LL edges in these cases, the trick is to **begin the algorithm in the direction of the unflipped edge**. You can incorporate this simple trick into your solving even if you are not learning ZB.

I hope these examples give you some insight into how the use of specialized algorithms can help you orient all the LL edges simultaneously when solving the F2L. The examples here are nothing special, just a few little tricks you can use in your solving. But be warned, ZB is **hard work**; just the sheer number of cases to learn is enough to put off most people.

The algorithms found so far for ZB cases are usually optimal, or just suboptimal, so while the move count may be short, they can sometimes be awkward and slow to perform. But like OLL + PLL, as more people work on this system, they will find better algorithms, and soon enough there will be a set of extremely fast, specialized ZB

■ **Table 6.17**
3×3×3 Expert Techniques—ZBF2L Examples: Using Moves to Your Advantage

Do y′ R′ U′ R U2 R′ U2 R d′ R U R′ U′ to set up.

Move: **R U′ R′ d R′ U2 R U2′ R′ U R**

Move: **U R U′ R′ d R′ U2 R U2′ R′ U R**

The same move is used to solve both cases, except the end result in the first example is that you have only 2 LL edges oriented correctly, and in the second example you have all 4! What happened? In the second example, a **setup move (U) is inserted at the beginning**, because this particular algorithm flips the FR and UF edges. So by **moving the unflipped LL edge into the UF position before executing the algorithm**, you will automatically orient all the edges. You can recognize and perform this maneuver in literally a fraction of a second; it's not a difficult trick, and it's worth knowing even if you are not learning ZB or VH.

algorithms. One of the best resources for ZBF2L algorithms is Lars Vandenbergh's speedcubing website; you can find the address in "Speedcubing Websites" at the end of this book.

CORNER ORIENT LAST LAYER (COLL)

The Corner Orient Last Layer algorithm set, or COLL, is an advanced last layer strategy. If, upon reaching the LL stage of your solution, the LL edges are already correctly oriented—achieved either by chance or by making use of some of the techniques described in the previous sections on influencing the LL during F2L—you can use the algorithms given in Table 6.18 to orient **and** permute the LL corners simultaneously.

The main advantage of continuing in this way is that it greatly increases your chance of skipping the PLL step altogether. You have 1 out of 12 chances of doing this, and the remaining 11 of the 12 times you leave yourself with a fast-edges-only permutation. However, the flip side is that the cases can be hard to recognize, the algorithms are quite long, and there are a lot of them! It is generally accepted that learning COLL isn't enough to directly improve your solving times significantly, but by learning these skills you may see improvements in other areas, especially in your ability to recognize cases quickly and remember lots of algorithms. This experience is good to get under your belt, especially if you are a sub-20 cuber on the lookout for anything that could shave fractions of a second off your times.

There are 40 cases, each identified by the orientation case and a 4-letter code. When identifying your COLL case, concentrate on the 6 stickers at ULB, URB, ULF, URF, FLU, and FRU. Only 4 of these stickers will be different colors than the color of your top face; these are the stickers that the 4-letter code refers to. The code is written in 2 columns of 2 letters; the left column corresponds to the ULB, ULF, and FLU stickers, and the right column corresponds to the URB, URF, and FRU stickers. If 2 stickers have the same color, they are designated the front color, by the letter F. The other colors are then assigned letters relating to their positions relative to the front color. So if the sticker in the position F was Red, then L would be a Blue sticker on your cube. If you are having trouble understanding this (which is not easy to explain on paper), simply do the inverse of 1 of the algorithms and see what the sticker pattern looks like. You should then be able to associate it with the corresponding 4-letter code.

3×3×3 Expert Techniques—Corner Orient Last Layer

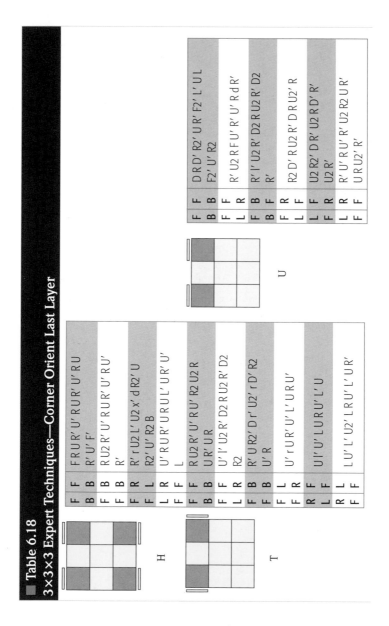

H

F F	F R U R' U' R U R' U' R U	
B B	R' U' F'	
F B	R U2 R' U' R U R' U'	
F B	R'	
F R	R' r U2 L' U2 x' d R2' U	
L F	R2' U' R2 B	
L R	U' R U R' U R U L' U R' U'	
F F	L	

T

F F	R U2 R' U' R U' R' R2 U2 R
B B	U R' U R
F F	U' l' U2 R' D2 R U2 R' D2
L R	R2
F B	R' U R2' D r' U2' r D' R2
F B	U' R
F L	U' r U R' U' L' U R U'
F R	
R F	U l' U' L U R U' L' U
L F	
R L	L U' L' U2' L R U' L' U R'
F F	

U

F F	D R D' R2' U R' F2' L' U L
B B	F2' U' R2
F B	R' U2 R F U' R' U' R d R'
L R	
F B	R' l' U2 R' D2 R U2 R' D2
B F	R'
F R	R2 D' R U2 R' D R U2' R
L F	
L F	U2 R2' D R' U2 R D' R'
F R	U2 R'
L R	R' l' R U' R' R' U2 R2 U R'
F F	U R U2' R'

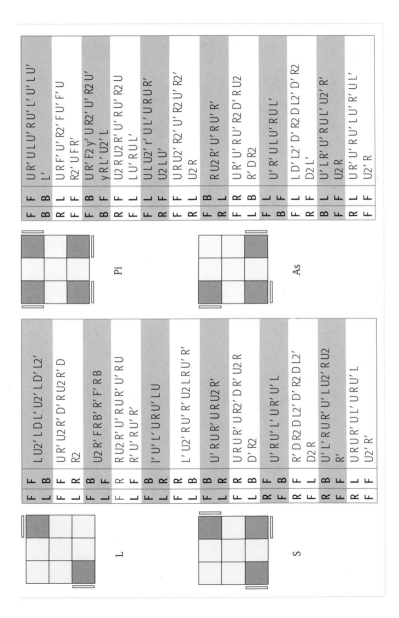

L

F	L	LU2'LDL'U2'LDL2'
F	B	
F	F	UR'U2R'D'RU2R'D
L	R	R2
F	B	U2R'FRB'R'F'RB
L	F	
F	R	RU2R'U'RUR'U'RU
L	F	R'U'R'
F	B	l'U'L'U'RU'LU
L	R	
F	R	L'U2'RU'R'U2LRU'R'
L	B	
F	L	U'RUR'URU2R'
L	R	
F	R	URUR'URU2'DR'U2R
L	B	D'R2
R	F	U'RU'L'U'RU'L
F	B	
R	F	R'DR2DL2'D'R2DL2'
F	L	D2R
R	B	U'L'RUR'U'LU2'RU2
F	F	R'
R	L	URUR'UL'URU'L
F	F	U2'R'

S

Pi

F	F	UR'ULU'RU'L'U'LU
B	B	L'
R	L	URF'U'R2'FU'F'U
F	F	R2'UFR'
F	B	UR'F2y'UR2'U'R2U'
B	F	yRL'U2'L
R	F	U2RU2R'U'RU'R2U
F	L	LU'RUL'
F	L	ULU2'r'UL'URUR'
R	F	U2LU'
F	F	U'RU2'R2'U'R2U'R2'
R	L	U2R
F	B	RU2R'U'RU'R'
F	R	U'R'U'RU'R2DR'RU2
L	B	R'DR2
F	L	U'R'ULU'RU'L'
B	F	
F	L	LD'L2'D'R2DL2'D'R2
R	F	D2L'
B	L	U'LR'U'RU'L'U2'R'
F	F	U2R
R	L	UR'U'RU'RU'LU'RU'L'
F	F	U2'R

As

ZBOROWSKI-BRUCHEM LAST LAYER (ZBLL)

The ZBLL is the closest speedcubers have come to a strategy that enables you to solve the last layer in 1 step, other than learning algorithms to solve the full set of 1,211 distinct LL cases. It is the natural finish to a solve that uses the ZBF2L; once you have reached the last layer step and you have influenced the LL edges such that they are all correctly oriented, there are now only 493 possible configurations (494 including the solved case). Knowing an algorithm for each case would allow you to solve the LL in 1 step. This is an extreme brute-force approach and requires a lot of dedication to learn; to date (2007), nobody has managed to learn the full set of cases for speedcubing.

Most speedcubers are in agreement that knowing and completely mastering the full system would allow you to take a second or 2 off your time, but to feel the benefit you would need to be a perfect cuber in all other areas. It is beyond the scope of this book to list algorithms for all of the cases; in fact, many of the cases do not have good algorithms yet. It is doubtful that ZBLL will become a system in wide use, but those who do manage to learn it may well achieve legendary status in the world of speedcubing.

COMBINING LAST LAYER TECHNIQUES

You can use the last layer techniques I have described in several different combinations to gradually improve your speedcubing. It's not necessary to always use ZBF2L with ZBLL; you can gradually build up your knowledge of both by learning VHF2L and COLL. Possible combinations include:

- The VH System: VHF2L + COLL + PLL (if necessary). This system was developed to be a stepping stone between standard CFOP and ZB. In the process, you do not learn anything extra that won't be useful if you decide to carry on and learn ZB. However, it is still a good system on its own.

- The ZB System: ZBF2L + ZBLL. This is the ultimate system, but mastery requires knowledge of 799 algorithms, which to date nobody has accomplished.
- Combination: VHF2L + ZBLL. This is a system I am currently working on, harnessing the power of the ZBLL with the ease of the VHF2L.
- Combination: ZBF2L + COLL + PLL (if necessary). This is another combination of systems, but it's only really useful if you intend to carry on and learn the full ZB. There is no real advantage to learning all 306 ZBF2L algorithms if you do not then go on to learn the ZBLL.

Any of the above approaches requires a lot of hard work and dedication, even more so than that needed to master the CFOP system. But if you have the time, the patience, and an overwhelming drive to improve your speedcubing, then give it a go! You could one day be the fastest speedcuber in the world. I wish you the best of luck for whichever path you decide to take from here, whether it's ZB or VH or you are just satisfied with trying to improve on your standard CFOP.

7

A Method to Solve Rubik's Revenge (4×4×4)

'll begin this chapter with a warning. Don't try to run before you can walk! If you want to attempt to solve the 4×4×4 before you have really tried to get a grip on the 3×3×3, that is fine, but since you are reading this chapter, I will assume that you want to learn a solution. This solution is geared toward cubers who already have some experience with the 3×3×3, have learned a solution (beginner or expert) or figured it out on their own, and can solve it from memory without any problems. If you are a complete novice to cubing, you may be able to follow the solution described in this section, but you will find it hard going compared with those who have experience already with the standard Rubik's Cube.

The 4×4×4, being larger than the standard 3×3×3, has an even greater number of possible configurations than the mighty 43 quintillion boasted by Rubik's Cube. In fact, the Rubik's Revenge has a staggering 7.4 quattuordecillion (that's 7.4×10^{45}) possible positions, and only 1 of them is the solution! The world's elite can solve this puzzle in about 60 seconds on average. At the time of writing, the current official world record is 46.63 seconds, set by Mátyás Kuti of Hungary at the UK Open Championships of 2007.

THINGS TO KNOW BEFORE YOU GET STARTED

Please familiarize yourself with the 4×4×4 notation used in this book by reading chapter 3, "Cubing Notation," before you attempt to learn this solution. It will immediately make things a lot easier for you.

The 4×4×4 is known as an "even" cube, because it has an even number of cubies along each dimension. This has some important consequences, 1 of which is that there are no fixed center pieces, meaning that there is no quick and fast way to determine where each color goes in relation to the others. Because of this, it's even more important than ever to **know your color scheme**. If your cube is scrambled already, and you don't know where each color should go, there is an easy way to determine the color scheme. Assuming that you can solve the corners of a 3×3×3 or solve a 2×2×2, simply solve the corners of your 4×4×4, so they look like Figure 7.1.

The evenness of the 4×4×4 also allows some particular cases to appear that are not possible to have on the 3×3×3. At first glance, this statement is obvious and unnecessary, but once you have read through the solution, this statement will become much more relevant.

The solution to the 4×4×4 relies a lot less on learning algorithms, but more emphasis is placed on a simple general procedure that you can apply to any scrambled 4×4×4. However, to solve it using the method below, you still must be able to solve a 3×3×3.

Figure 7.1 With the corners solved, you can easily see which center should go where.

OVERVIEW OF THE 3×3×3 REDUCTION METHOD

The strategy that is in use to varying degrees by most of the world's elite is known as the 3×3×3 reduction method. The idea is to take your scrambled 4×4×4 cube, transform it into the equivalent of a 3×3×3 cube, and then solve it using a 3×3×3 method. While more direct solutions are available, this solution has proven to be 1 of the fastest and most widely used solutions in speedcubing. It is also quite easy to follow, especially if you have previous experience in solving the 3×3×3.

The 3×3×3 reduction method works like this:

- **Solve the center pieces:** By solving the 24 pieces that make up the centers, ensuring they are in the correct relative positions according to your cube's color scheme, you will have formed the equivalent of the fixed center of a 3×3×3.

- **Pair up the double edges ("dedges"):** By matching up edge pieces that have the same color (there are 12 pairs of 2 edges that have the same color), you form the equivalent of 1 large edge on the 3×3×3.

- **Solve the resultant 3×3×3 cube:** Now you can solve the cube in the same way as the 3×3×3, making sure to turn only the outer layers to preserve the centers and edges. You may come up against some strange cases when attempting to solve the last layer, however, and you will need to know some new tricks to overcome these. I describe these in more detail in the "Orientation Parity" and "Permutation Parity" sections.

Now that you know the idea behind the solution, let's proceed to the actual solution!

SOLVING THE CENTERS

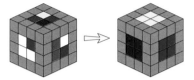

Solving the centers is straightforward, but it can take a little time to really get your head around it. It is much like solving the 3×3×3 Cross stage. You have the freedom of the whole cube at this point, since nothing has been solved. There are 24 center pieces on the 4×4×4, 4 on each of the 6 faces; you'll know them because they have only 1 sticker. In the following section I describe a simple beginner solution that is rigid and easy to follow, with only 1 simple procedure to learn. I'll refer to the terms centers and center cubies, which describe the simulated 3×3×3 center and actual 4×4×4 centers, respectively.

Choose a color to start with. It is a good idea to choose the color that is most complete already—for example, if 3 White center cubies are already together, then you have to add only 1 more to complete the whole center. However, once you get used to solving the centers, you might find it easier to always start with the same color, because then you will get used to where the other centers must go relative to the first center.

Solving the First Center

Solving the first center is very much like solving the Cross stage on the 3×3×3. There are no set algorithms, and it is very much an intuitive step. There are some guidelines that you can follow, however, to help you complete this first step. The best way is to first match up 2 of your chosen color center cubies so that they form a 2×1 block. Next, do the same with the remaining 2 center cubies, but make sure you don't break up the first block. Finally, join them together to make a 2×2 block, which is a complete center. Table 7.1 should make this process clearer.

■ **Table 7.1**
4×4×4—Solving the First Center: Example

 This is the initial position in our example. The first thing to do is to make a matching 2×1 block. Do this with the moves:

F (D d)
(Reminder: Lowercase letters mean you need to shift the second layer in from that face, not the outer 2 like the 3×3×3. Refer to page 11.)

 With 1 matching 2×1 block, you can pair up the remaining 2 center cubies. Be careful not to upset the block you have already solved. Do this by:

U2 (R r)

 All that remains is to join the blocks together to form a center. This can be accomplished in this example by:

R′ (F′ f′)

 Here is the finished center.

Hold the cube so that the completed first center is on the bottom face. Now you are ready to complete the remaining 5 centers.

Solving the Remaining Centers

Here it becomes very important to know your cube's color scheme. Now that you have solved 1 center and are holding the cube with that center on the bottom, you already have enough information to know which color should be on the top face. You still have a free choice about where the other 4 centers should go around the middle layers, so it is a good idea to see if any centers are almost completed. If a face has 2 or 3 Blue center cubies, for example, then solve the Blue center on this face.

The strategy here is to swap the Ufr center cubie (the center cubie on the **U**-layer at the intersection of the **f** and **r** slices) with the Ful center cubie. By preparing the ground each time before a swap, you can gradually build up all of the centers with this simple move. Table 7.2 explains the process.

Table 7.3 should shed some light on this procedure. Although it may seem a bit awkward at first, in reality it is very straightforward. The only thing to be careful of is to make sure that you think about which pieces you are swapping.

By swapping the centers in this way, you will eventually build all 5 centers. If you get to a position where your top center is complete but some other centers aren't, then hold the cube so an unsolved center cubie is on the front in the Ful position and swap this with a random piece from the U-face. You will then have a different center cubie on the U-face to solve.

Read the swapping procedure notes and example carefully, and experiment with the swapping move to see how it works. With a little bit of practice, you will get the hang of it, and once you do, you will always be able to solve the centers with this simple move.

■ Table 7.2
4×4×4—Solving the Final 5 Centers

Move: (R′ r′) F (R r)

- Turn the U-layer so that a center cubie that isn't the color of the top center (that is, the color that goes opposite the color of your first center, which is on the bottom) is in the Ufr position (see diagram).
- Turn the bottom 3 layers to bring the face onto which you are going to solve the center cubie to the front.
- Make sure that you are swapping with a center cubie of a different color (you may need to turn the F-face).
- Apply the swapping algorithm.
- Repeat from the beginning until all centers are solved.

■ Table 7.3
4×4×4—Solving the Final 5 Centers Example: Swapping 2 Center Cubies

You have already solved the White center, and you are holding it on the bottom. When solved, the up center will therefore be Yellow. A Blue center cubie is in Ufr, so this is the one to solve next. There are 2 Blue center cubies on the front face, so it makes sense to solve the Blue center here. When you make this choice, it fixes the other centers, so as you look at the diagram, Red will be on the right, Green on the back, and Orange on the left. If you applied the swapping move now, you would be swapping a Blue center cubie with a Blue center cubie, and this would get you nowhere. You therefore have to turn the F-face first to get a cubie that is not Blue into the Ful position.

Move: F

Now everything is set to perform the swap.

Move: **(R′ r′) F (R r)**

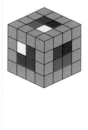

The swap is complete. The Blue center is nearing completion, and you have a new center cubie in Ufr. In this example, it is Yellow, which actually belongs on the U-face, so you wouldn't want to swap that with anything. Before making another swap, you would have to turn the U-layer to bring a different cubie into Ufr (for example, **U** would allow you to swap a Red center cubie, and then you would move **(u d′ D′)** to bring the Red center to the Front).

In Case of Mistakes

Even if you know your cube's color scheme, it's possible to get the centers in the wrong positions with respect to each other, especially when you are a beginner. The algorithms shown in Tables 7.4 and 7.5 can get you out of this situation and restore the correct positions of your centers.

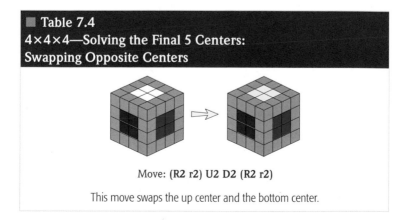

■ Table 7.4
4×4×4—Solving the Final 5 Centers:
Swapping Opposite Centers

Move: **(R2 r2) U2 D2 (R2 r2)**

This move swaps the up center and the bottom center.

■ **Table 7.5**
4×4×4—Solving the Final 5 Centers:
Swapping Adjacent Centers

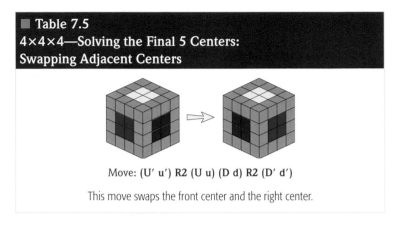

Move: (U′ u′) R2 (U u) (D d) R2 (D′ d′)

This move swaps the front center and the right center.

Now that your centers are solved, you are halfway there. Next you must pair up the dedges to complete the 3×3×3 reduction phase of the solution. This is covered in the following section.

PAIRING UP THE DOUBLE EDGES (DEDGES)

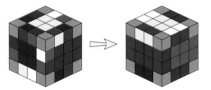

The first thing to do is decide on a color to hold on the bottom. Once you have chosen it, try to always hold the cube so this color is on the bottom for the first stage of pairing up the dedges. Divide the cube into 3 sections: the top layer, the bottom layer, and the layers in between. The idea is to pair up edges in the middle layers and store them in the top and bottom layers.

The First 4 Dedges

Look at the edge piece at uFL. This is the top edge of the 2 edges at the front and left position. Find the other edge that has the same colors as this edge, and then use Table 7.6 below to see which situation you have. Once you have identified the case, use the appropriate algorithms to solve it.

If you have applied the correct algorithm, the other edge piece will now be at dFR. To pair up the edges into a dedge, simply apply the move **(D′ d′)**, as shown in Table 7.7.

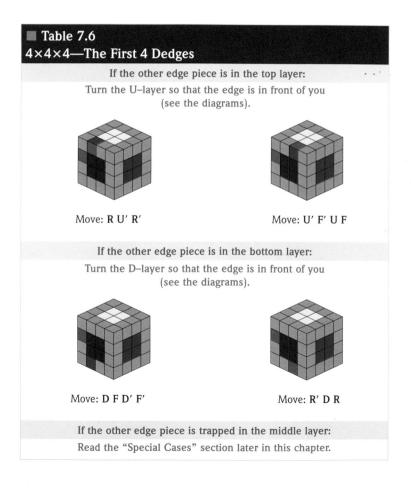

■ **Table 7.6**
4×4×4—The First 4 Dedges

If the other edge piece is in the top layer:

Turn the U–layer so that the edge is in front of you
(see the diagrams).

Move: **R U′ R′**   Move: **U′ F′ U F**

If the other edge piece is in the bottom layer:

Turn the D–layer so that the edge is in front of you
(see the diagrams).

Move: **D F D′ F′**   Move: **R′ D R**

If the other edge piece is trapped in the middle layer:

Read the "Special Cases" section later in this chapter.

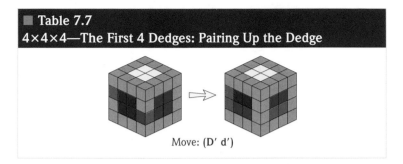

Move: (D′ d′)

Now that you have paired up the dedge, you need to store it out of the way so that you don't accidentally break it up again at a later stage. We will store the first 4 dedges in the U-layer, using the moves in Table 7.8.

■ **Table 7.8**
4×4×4—The First 4 Dedges:
Storing the Dedge in the U-Layer

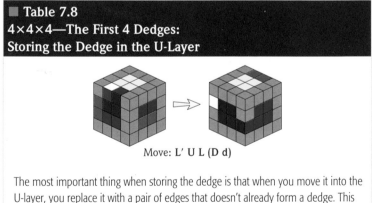

Move: L′ U L (D d)

The most important thing when storing the dedge is that when you move it into the U-layer, you replace it with a pair of edges that doesn't already form a dedge. This storing move replaces the pair of edges at UF, so before you store the dedge, **you must turn the U-layer to bring a pair of unsolved edges to the front.** At first, it is likely (but not necessarily) the case that you have 4 pairs of unsolved edges in the U-layer. But as you fix more dedges and store them in the U-layer, you have fewer positions available. At this point, you must be really careful to not break up dedges you have already formed and stored out of the way.

Also remember to add the **(D d)** move at the end of the storing move. This restores the centers that were broken up during the pair-up phase.

At the same time that you store your solved dedge, you place a new unpaired edge at uFL, and you can begin the process again. Repeat until all 4 dedge positions in the U-layer contain solved dedges, at which point you can no longer use the U-layer for storing.

The Next 4 Dedges

There is nothing new to learn for this step. **Simply turn the cube upside down (z2)** and solve the next 4 dedges in exactly the same way as the first 4.

Special Cases

When the other edge piece is trapped in the middle layer, the trick is to first move it into the U-layer and then solve it using the procedure described previously in the "First 4 Dedges" section. Table 7.9 shows you how.

Solving the Final 4 Dedges

At this stage we have solved 8 dedges and stored them in the U- and D-layers. Both these layers are now full, so we can't use the tricks we used for the first 8 dedges to solve the final 4.

We begin to solve the remaining dedges in exactly the same way as before, starting with the edge in the uFL position. We then search for the other edge that has the same colors, as before. By now there are only 4 possible positions that the other edge could be in. Table 7.10 shows the 4 cases and what you should do for each one.

The object of Table 7.10 is to get the other edge into the FR position. The next step is to make sure that the other edge occupies the uFR position. If it already does, then we can finally complete the dedge, but if it instead occupies the dFR position, we must flip the edge pair first, shown in Table 7.11.

■ Table 7.9
4×4×4—Solving the Dedges: Special Case

When the edge piece is trapped in the middle layer:

Rotate the cube around the *y*-axis to bring the other
edge piece to the FR position.

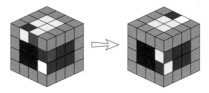

Move: **R U′ R′**

In this case, the other edge piece you want is the Blue/Orange (or it could equally
be the White/Blue). It is trapped in the middle layer, so you rotate the cube to
bring it to the FR position. Applying the move **R U′ R′** moves the edge you want
into the U-layer, where you can solve it using 1 of the standard procedures. As
with the storing move, **you must be careful that the edge pair you replace in
the U-layer is not a solved dedge**, so you may have to turn the U-layer to bring a
random unsolved pair into the UF position (in this case, the Blue/Yellow +
Yellow/Orange pair). Finally, rotate the cube back again and solve the dedge in
the normal way.

Once you have manipulated the cube so that the other edge is in
the uFR position, you can finally solve the dedge using the maneuver
shown in Table 7.12.

When the dedge is solved, rotate the cube clockwise around the *y*-
axis to bring the next edge pair into the FL position. You can then repeat
the same procedure to solve the tenth and eleventh dedges, the only
difference being that for each iteration there will be 1 less position in
which the "other edge" can initially be. When you have solved the
eleventh dedge, the twelfth dedge is automatically solved, and you have
completed the 3×3×3 reduction phase of the solution.

■ Table 7.10
4×4×4—The Final 4 Dedges

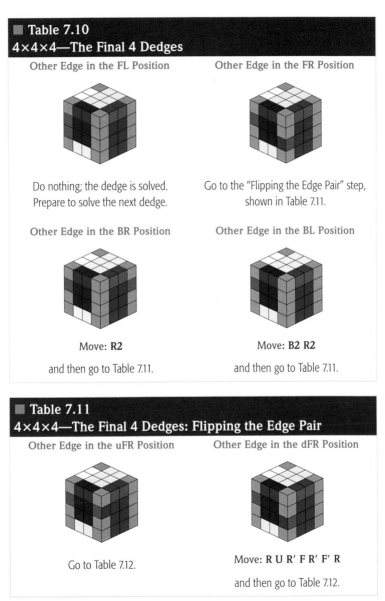

Other Edge in the FL Position

Do nothing; the dedge is solved.
Prepare to solve the next dedge.

Other Edge in the FR Position

Go to the "Flipping the Edge Pair" step,
shown in Table 7.11.

Other Edge in the BR Position

Move: **R2**

and then go to Table 7.11.

Other Edge in the BL Position

Move: **B2 R2**

and then go to Table 7.11.

■ Table 7.11
4×4×4—The Final 4 Dedges: Flipping the Edge Pair

Other Edge in the uFR Position

Go to Table 7.12.

Other Edge in the dFR Position

Move: **R U R′ F R′ F′ R**

and then go to Table 7.12.

■ **Table 7.12**
4×4×4—The Final 4 Dedges: Final Step

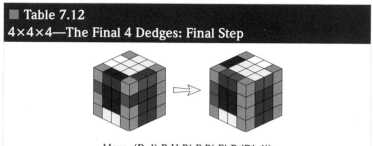

Move: **(D d) R U R′ F R′ F′ R (D′ d′)**

This algorithm is more or less exactly the same as the previous algorithm for flipping the edge, but with some extra slice moves. The dFR edge is replaced by the dFL edge, then the FR edge pair is flipped upside down, so the uFR edge becomes the dFR edge. When the slice move is undone, the centers are restored, and the dFR edge goes back to being the dFL edge.

SOLVING THE REDUCED 3×3×3 CUBE

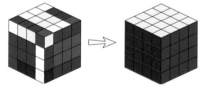

Now that you have simulated a 3×3×3 on your 4×4×4, you can begin to solve it like a 3×3×3. Turning only the outer layers will ensure that your centers and edges stay intact, and you can use exactly the same solution you know for the 3×3×3 to complete the 4×4×4. However, you should be aware of a couple of scenarios and know how to deal with them. Although you are simulating a 3×3×3, it is actually still a 4×4×4, and things that are possible in the 4×4×4 reference frame are impossible in the 3×3×3 reference frame. These 2 instances are called *parities*, and they will become apparent once you reach the last layer stage. I cover the algorithms for dealing with them in the next 2 sections.

ORIENTATION PARITY

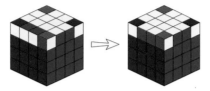

Reducing the 4×4×4 into a pseudo-3×3×3 in this way gives you a 50-50 chance of having an odd number of dedge flips. This will become more apparent by the time you have solved the F2L (really F3L!) and are proceeding to solve the orientation of the last layer. On the 3×3×3, it is only possible at this stage to have 0, 2, or 4 edges correctly flipped, but the 4×4×4 makes it possible for your 3×3×3 equivalent to have any number of dedges flipped, from 0 to all 4. If you have an even number of dedge flips, you can continue to solve in the normal way. However, if you have an odd number of dedge flips, you need to apply an "orientation parity fix" algorithm to restore what is known as "even parity." The orientation parity fix flips over a single dedge, but be careful to apply it correctly, or else you might end up going back to square 1— a scrambled mess!

To fix the orientation parity, choose from 1 of the algorithms in Table 7.13; try them out to see which you like best. The first set of algorithms changes only the orientation of a single dedge, whereas the second set changes the orientation of a single dedge plus 2 corner pieces. Although the algorithms in the second set look longer, they tend to be faster for speedcubing since they use a lot of double layer turns instead of inner slice turns. You can use any of these algorithms to fix the orientation

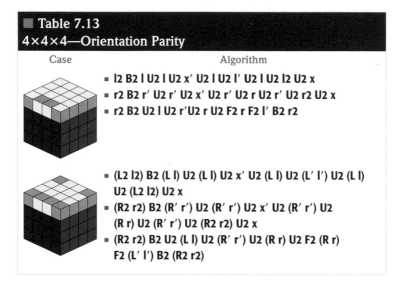

■ **Table 7.13**
4×4×4—Orientation Parity

Case	Algorithm
	■ l2 B2 l U2 l U2 x' U2 l U2 l' U2 l U2 l2 U2 x
	■ r2 B2 r' U2 r' U2 x' U2 r' U2 r U2 r' U2 r2 U2 x
	■ r2 B2 U2 l U2 r'U2 r U2 F2 r F2 l' B2 r2
	■ (L2 l2) B2 (L l) U2 (L l) U2 x' U2 (L l) U2 (L' l') U2 (L l) U2 (L2 l2) U2 x
	■ (R2 r2) B2 (R' r') U2 (R' r') U2 x' U2 (R' r') U2 (R r) U2 (R' r') U2 (R2 r2) U2 x
	■ (R2 r2) B2 U2 (L l) U2 (R' r') U2 (R r) U2 F2 (R r) F2 (L' l') B2 (R2 r2)

parity, but bear in mind that in addition to fixing the parity, they affect other pieces in the last layer. This is why fixing your orientation parity should be the first thing you do when solving the last layer.

PERMUTATION PARITY

There is also a 50-50 chance of having a permutation parity error once you have fixed the orientation of the last layer. By the time you reach the permutation step on the 3×3×3, the total number of edge swaps and corner swaps will be an even number. But because we are solving an even cube, it is possible, when solving the 4×4×4 using the 3×3×3

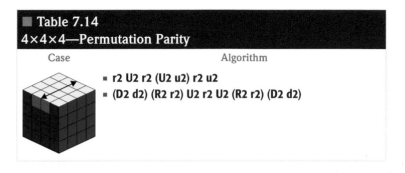

■ **Table 7.14**
4×4×4—Permutation Parity

Case	Algorithm
	■ **r2 U2 r2 (U2 u2) r2 u2**
	■ **(D2 d2) (R2 r2) U2 r2 U2 (R2 r2) (D2 d2)**

reduction method, that the total number of swaps needed appears to be an odd number. This isn't so easy to recognize, but if you encounter a case that you cannot solve using your normal 3×3×3 method, then you have a permutation parity error. Table 7.14 shows you what to do.

TIPS FOR GETTING FASTER

The method described in this chapter is a great system for solving your Revenge. While it is simple to do, it is also not very efficient. To solve the 4×4×4 fast, as with any other twisty puzzle, you must use an efficient solution and be able to execute it quickly.

Faster Centers

Most speedcubers solve the centers in a certain order to ensure their color scheme is always correct. The first center can be solved in much the same way as described above, but speedcubers can usually see the shortest solution to this center. Next they solve the opposite center and then the remaining 4 centers, 1 after the other, using special tricks and knowledge of the fastest way to solve the last 2 centers. By solving in this way, it is possible to reduce your move count to about 30 for the centers, and if you execute it at 2 to 3 turns per second, times of 10 to 15 seconds for the centers are possible. The top speedcubers solve the centers of the 4×4×4 in about 10 to 12 seconds.

■ Table 7.15
4×4×4—Faster Centers Example

Scramble with Yellow on top and Red on front: B L2 u F2 R′ D2 R2
u2 L2 B2 f2 F R B f2 L2 r2 R2 f D′ u2 U′ B2 F L′ r R u L′ F2

First center (White):
- **U′ (R r) (D′ d′) U′ (L′ l′)**

Second (opposite) center (Yellow):
- **x2 u′ U2 (R r) U2 (R′ r′)**

Third center (Orange):
- **z x′ U′ (R′ r′)**

Fourth center (Green):
- **x′ U (R′ r′) U′ F′ (R r) F x′ U (R2 r2) U2 (R2 r2)**

Fifth and sixth centers (Red and Blue):
- **F (R r) U′ (R′ r′) U (R r) U2 (R′ r′)**

Table 7.15 shows how a speedcuber might solve the centers, which should give you some ideas for improving your center-solving skills. Scramble a solved 4×4×4 using the example scramble in the table. Take great care when applying the scramble, and make sure the end result looks like the diagram; otherwise, the solution will not solve the centers.

Faster Dedges

There are 2 dominant advanced strategies for solving the dedges: the 2-pair system and the 6-pair system. As the names suggest, the goal of each system is to solve not 1 dedge at a time but rather 2 or 6 dedges simultaneously. Each system has its advantages and disadvantages. The 6-pair system can be more efficient but has a greater chance of encountering some awkward cases, whereas the 2-pair system may be less efficient in terms of numbers of moves but more straightforward to execute. The 6-pair system is simply an extension of the 2-pair system, so I'll discuss the 2-pair system and let you work out the 6-pair system for yourself.

2-Pair System

The 2-pair and 6-pair strategies work on a principle similar to the beginner method, except that you must be more careful about where you store a solved dedge. Rather than storing it in a random position in the U-layer, you store it in such a way that it brings a useful edge piece into the middle layers.

First of all, solve 2 dedges and store them at BR and BL. This leaves 10 dedges to solve, 4 in the U-layer, 4 in the D-layer, and 2 at FL and FR. Then pair up dedges in the front 2 slots and store them in both the U-layer and the D-layer. Follow the example shown in Table 7.16.

You can encounter 1 or 2 difficult cases at the end of the dedge-pairing process, but I'll leave it as an exercise for you to find simple solutions to these problems, using what you already know. I will give you a clue: the "flip" procedure once again comes in very handy.

Faster 3×3×3 Phase

The amount of time required to solve the 3×3×3 phase is mainly dependent on the method you use to solve a 3×3×3. If you use a beginner method, you will naturally need more time to complete the 3×3×3 phase than someone who uses the CFOP system with some advanced techniques. Improving this stage is all about using a fast method, practicing a lot, and getting good at recognizing and fixing the orientation and permutation parity problems described earlier.

Table 7.16
4×4×4—Faster Dedges Example

Begin by looking at the edge at uFL, as before. In the diagram, this is the Green/Red piece (the Red sticker is not visible on the diagram). The other Green/Red edge is at rUF, and you insert it into dFR.

Move: **U′ F′ U F**

Get ready to make the first dedge. **(U′ u′)** will do the job, but before you do that, note the colors on the edge at uFR. When you make the pair, you are going to store it in such a way that the other edge with the uFR colors (Blue/White) is brought down into dFR. The other Blue/White edge is at the moment at lUF.

Move: **u′ R U′ R′**

The first dedge is stored in the U-layer, inserted there to bring the other Blue/White edge into dFR. Now, when you restore the centers, you make another dedge at FR.

Move: **(U u)**

Having formed another dedge, store it so that the other Orange/White edge moves into dFR. Then just repeat this procedure, each time forming 2 pairs, until all dedges are solved.

8

A Method to Solve Rubik's Professor Cube (5×5×5)

As with the 4×4×4 solution, this solution is geared toward cubers who already have some experience with the 3×3×3, have learned a solution (beginner or expert) or figured it out on their own, and can solve it from memory without any problems. If you are a complete novice to cubing, you may be able to follow the solution described in this section, but you will find it hard going compared with those who have experience with the standard Rubik's Cube.

The 5×5×5 is a monster, packing in a phenomenal 280 trevigintillion (2.8×10^{72}) possible configurations. It is currently the largest cubical twisty puzzle in production. The best 5×5×5 solvers in the world can complete this puzzle in about 120 seconds; the current world record is 90.58 seconds, set by Hungarian Mátyás Kuti at the UK Open Championships of 2007.

THINGS TO KNOW BEFORE YOU GET STARTED

Once again, please familiarize yourself with the notation used in this book by reading chapter 3, "Cubing Notation," before attempting to learn this solution. Otherwise, it won't make a great deal of sense to you.

The 5×5×5 shares the same characteristic of fixed centers with the 3×3×3; if you open up a 5×5×5, you will see that the center pieces are joined together in the core of the puzzle. This means that, unlike the 4×4×4, the colors of the faces are determined by the colors of the center pieces.

The 5×5×5 has many different types of pieces. Table 8.1 describes the naming scheme of each type of piece, and I recommend that you learn these before attempting to solve the cube. It will make your life a lot easier.

THE GENERAL STRATEGY

We will expand on the 3×3×3 reduction method we used to solve the 4×4×4 and apply the same principles to the 5×5×5. Again, there are more direct ways to solve, but 3×3×3 reduction is the method of choice for nearly all today's speedcubers.

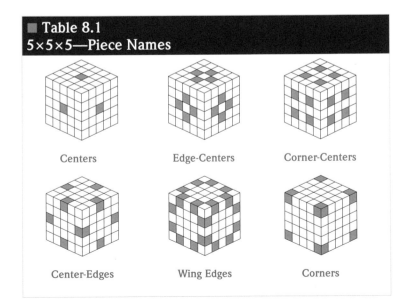

■ **Table 8.1**
5×5×5—Piece Names

| Centers | Edge-Centers | Corner-Centers |
| Center-Edges | Wing Edges | Corners |

Applied to the 5×5×5, the 3×3×3 reduction method works like this:

- **Solve the center pieces:** There are 54 center cubies to solve, 9 on each face. The center on each face of the 5×5×5 determines the color that face will be. When solved, they form the equivalent of the center piece on a 3×3×3.

- **Pair up the triple edges (tredges):** By matching up edge pieces that have the same colors (there are 12 pairs of 3 edges that have the same colors), you form the equivalent of 1 large edge on the 3×3×3.

- **Solve the resultant 3×3×3 cube:** Now solve the cube in the same way as the 3×3×3, making sure to turn only the outer layers to preserve the centers and edges. There is only 1 special parity case that may occur on the 5×5×5, unlike the 2 that can occur on the 4×4×4.

SOLVING THE CENTERS

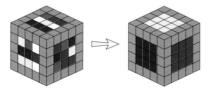

In this section I show you a simple procedure to solve the centers. Read through carefully a few times, following with your cube. It won't be long before you get the hang of it. We will solve a center at a time, rotating the cube as we do, so that we always solve the top center. By doing it this way, we gradually build up the centers without having to learn too much.

Choose a center to start with—it can be any color—and hold the cube so that your chosen center is on top. First of all, we will solve the edge-centers, shown in Table 8.2.

After solving the edge-centers, you need to solve the corner-centers to complete the up center. Table 8.3 shows you how.

After solving the corner-centers, the up center will be complete. **To solve the remaining 5 centers, simply rotate the cube to put an unsolved center on top, and repeat the procedures described above.**

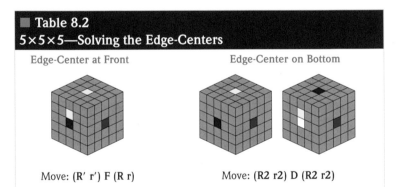

■ Table 8.2
5×5×5—Solving the Edge-Centers

Edge-Center at Front	Edge-Center on Bottom
Move: (R′ r′) F (R r)	Move: (R2 r2) D (R2 r2)

Find an edge-center somewhere on the cube that is the same color as your chosen color. While making sure that your chosen center color is on top, rotate the cube in your hands so that the edge-center is on either the front face or the down face.

Turn the up face so that an **unsolved edge-center is at Ur** (the position directly to the right of dead center). Turn the front face so that the edge-center of your chosen color is at Fu, or if it is on the down face, turn the down face so that the chosen edge-center is at Df (see the diagrams).

Apply the appropriate algorithm to solve the edge-center onto the up face.

Repeat this procedure until you have solved all 4 edge-centers on the up face.

■ Table 8.3
5×5×5—Solving the Corner-Centers

Corner-Center at Front	Corner-Center on Bottom

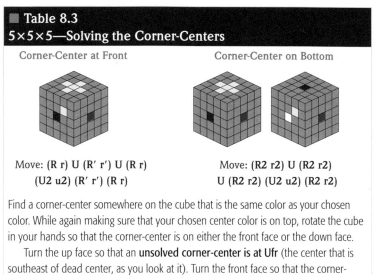

| Move: **(R r) U (R′ r′) U (R r)** | Move: **(R2 r2) U (R2 r2)** |
| **(U2 u2) (R′ r′) (R r)** | **U (R2 r2) (U2 u2) (R2 r2)** |

Find a corner-center somewhere on the cube that is the same color as your chosen color. While again making sure that your chosen center color is on top, rotate the cube in your hands so that the corner-center is on either the front face or the down face.

Turn the up face so that an **unsolved corner-center is at Ufr** (the center that is southeast of dead center, as you look at it). Turn the front face so that the corner-center of your chosen color is at Fur, or if it is on the down face, turn the down face so that the chosen edge-center is at Dfr (see the diagrams).

Apply the appropriate algorithm to solve the corner-center onto the up face.

Repeat this procedure until you have solved all 4 corner-centers on the up face.

SOLVING THE TRIPLE EDGES (TREDGES)

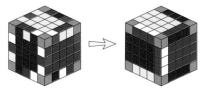

In principle, the solution is exactly the same as the 4×4×4. Choose a color to hold on the bottom and try to always hold the cube so this color is on the bottom. Divide the cube into 3 sections: the top layer, the bottom layer, and the layers in between. The idea is to pair up edges in the middle layers and store them in the top and bottom layers.

Important: When solving the tredges, don't be concerned about what happens to the centers. Although they are broken up, it is not necessary to restore them until you have solved 8 of the 12 tredges.

Solving the First 4 Tredges

Identify the wing edge at uLF. The cube has another wing edge with exactly the same colors; you need to find this and pair it up with the wing edge at uLF. Table 8.4 will help you figure out which situation you have and how to solve it.

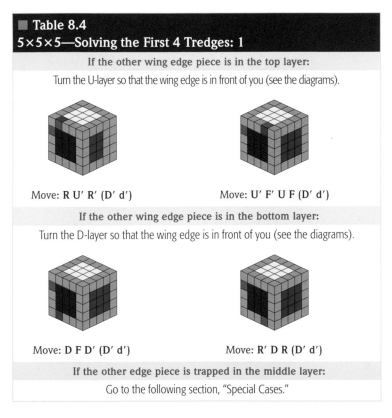

◼ **Table 8.4**
5×5×5—Solving the First 4 Tredges: 1

If the other wing edge piece is in the top layer:

Turn the U-layer so that the wing edge is in front of you (see the diagrams).

Move: **R U' R' (D' d')**   Move: **U' F' U F (D' d')**

If the other wing edge piece is in the bottom layer:

Turn the D-layer so that the wing edge is in front of you (see the diagrams).

Move: **D F D' (D' d')**   Move: **R' D R (D' d')**

If the other edge piece is trapped in the middle layer:

Go to the following section, "Special Cases."

Once you have paired up the wing edges, you need to match them up with the corresponding center-edge to form a tredge. Look around the cube to find the center-edge that has the same colors as the wing edge you just paired up. When you find it, use Table 8.5 to help you add it to the wing edges.

■ **Table 8.5**
5×5×5—Solving the First 4 Tredges: 2

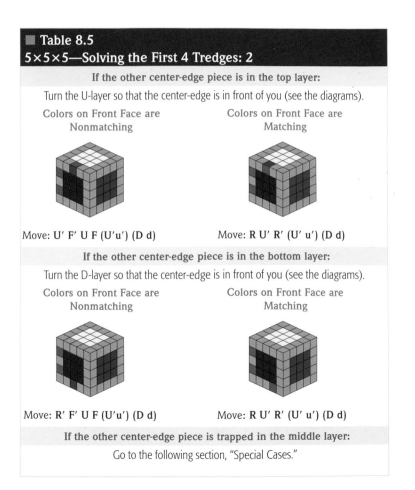

If the other center-edge piece is in the top layer:

Turn the U-layer so that the center-edge is in front of you (see the diagrams).

Colors on Front Face are Nonmatching	Colors on Front Face are Matching
Move: **U′ F′ U F (U′u′) (D d)**	Move: **R U′ R′ (U′ u′) (D d)**

If the other center-edge piece is in the bottom layer:

Turn the D-layer so that the center-edge is in front of you (see the diagrams).

Colors on Front Face are Nonmatching	Colors on Front Face are Matching
Move: **R′ F′ U F (U′u′) (D d)**	Move: **R U′ R′ (U′ u′) (D d)**

If the other center-edge piece is trapped in the middle layer:

Go to the following section, "Special Cases."

Now that you have paired up the tredge, you need to store it safely out of the way so that you don't break it up later on. We will store the first 4 tredges in the U-layer, in exactly the same way as we did with the 4×4×4. Table 8.6 shows you how.

Special Cases

Occasionally, a wing edge or center-edge that you seek is trapped in the middle layers. To solve this, rotate the cube in your hand, keeping your top and bottom faces the same, until the trapped piece is in the FR position. Then use the algorithm in Table 8.6 to move the trapped piece into the U-layer and replace it with a random piece. You must make sure—as with the storing move—that a random, unsolved tredge is in

---

■ **Table 8.6**
5×5×5—Solving the First 4 Tredges:
Storing the Tredge in the U-Layer

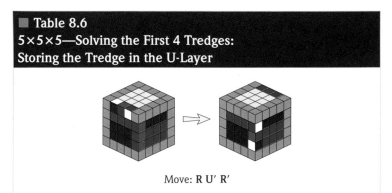

Move: **R U' R'**

The most important thing to be sure of when storing the tredge is that you replace it with a trio of edges that doesn't already form a tredge. This storing move replaces the pair of edges at UF, so before you store the tredge, you must turn the U-layer to bring a trio of unsolved edges to the front. At first, it is likely to be (but not necessarily) the case that you have 4 trios of unsolved edges in the U-layer. But as you fix more tredges and store them in the U-layer, you have fewer positions available. Then, you must be really careful to not break up tredges you have already formed and stored out of the way.

the UF position before swapping the pieces over. Once you have moved the trapped piece into the U-layer, you can use 1 of the moves given in the tables above to make the tredge.

Solving the Next 4 Tredges

When you have solved the first 4 tredges, the U-layer becomes full and can no longer hold any more solved tredges. To solve the next 4 tredges, as with the 4×4×4, simply rotate the cube upside down—so the D-layer becomes the new U-layer—and begin to fill it up again. You can use exactly the same procedure described above to solve the next 4 tredges, and again, **don't worry about the centers for now**.

Solving the Last 4 Tredges

At this point, we must restore the broken centers. This should be a simple case of turning the u and d slices. If this is not enough to fix your centers, then I am afraid you have gone wrong somewhere and will have to start again.

Before we go any further, Table 8.7 shows you an important move. This move to flip over a tredge is very useful at this stage (notice that it is exactly the same as the 4×4×4). You must learn this move since the next few steps rely heavily on it.

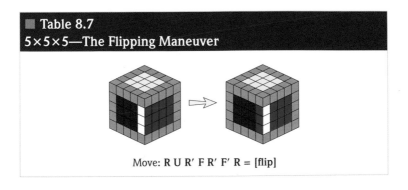

Table 8.7
5×5×5—The Flipping Maneuver

Move: R U R′ F R′ F′ R = [flip]

■ **Table 8.8**
5×5×5—Solving the Final 4 Tredges: 1

A wing edge in the FL position	A wing edge in the FR Position
If the colors do not match up, search for the other wing edge. If both wing edges are in FL, go to Table 8.10.	Go to Table 8.9.
A wing Edge in the BR Position	A Wing Edge in the BL Position
Move: **R2** and then go to Table 8.9.	Move: **B2 R2** and then go to Table 8.9.

To solve the remaining tredges, identify the colors of the FL center-edge. Look on the FR, BR, and BL edges for a wing edge that has the same colors. Once you find 1 of the 2 wing edges with the same colors, follow the directions in Table 8.8.

Table 8.9 shows how to pair it up with the center-edge.

Special Cases

If you get a case where both wing edges are in the FL position but the colors don't match with the center-edge, then don't worry. Table 8.10 shows a simple way to solve the tredge.

■ Table 8.9
5×5×5—Solving the Final 4 Tredges: 2

If the colors on the front face match:

Wing Edge is at dFR   Wing Edge is at uFR

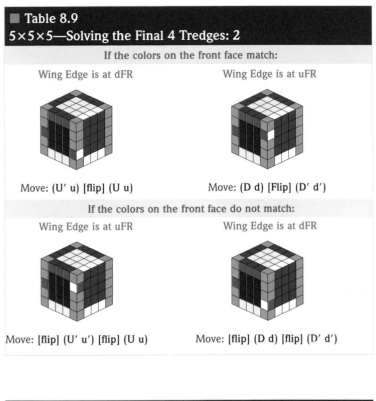

Move: (U′ u) [flip] (U u)   Move: (D d) [Flip] (D′ d′)

If the colors on the front face do not match:

Wing Edge is at uFR   Wing Edge is at dFR

Move: [flip] (U′ u′) [flip] (U u)   Move: [flip] (D d) [flip] (D′ d′)

■ Table 8.10
5×5×5—Solving the Final 4 Tredges:
Special Case

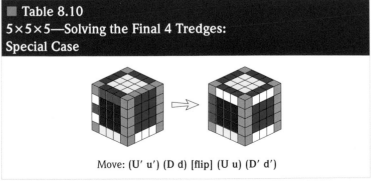

Move: (U′ u′) (D d) [flip] (U u) (D′ d′)

You must repeat the above procedure twice per tredge, because there are 2 wing edges to solve each time, and you must solve 3 tredges in this way. When you have solved 1 tredge, simply rotate the cube clockwise about the *y*-axis to bring another unsolved tredge into the FL position, ready to solve.

The Final Tredge

In 50% of solves, the twelfth and final tredge will be solved after you have solved the eleventh tredge. But in the other 50%, you must do some extra work to solve the final tredge. The problem—2 wing edges appear to be flipped over—is the same as the 4×4×4 orientation parity, and you can solve it in much the same way, as shown in Table 8.11.

Once you have fixed the final tredge, you have successfully completed the 3×3×3 reduction phase of the solution. You are only a few steps away from the completed 5×5×5 cube.

■ Table 8.11
5×5×5—The Final Tredge

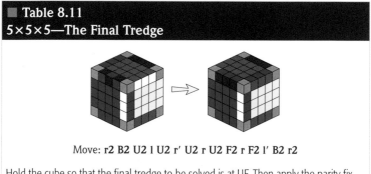

Move: **r2 B2 U2 l U2 r′ U2 r U2 F2 r F2 l′ B2 r2**

Hold the cube so that the final tredge to be solved is at UF. Then apply the parity fix given above. It is a long and not very nice move; even I forget this sometimes!

SOLVING THE REDUCED 3×3×3 CUBE

By turning the outer layers only, you can now solve the cube in exactly the same way as a 3×3×3. If you don't know how to solve the 3×3×3, please see the beginner method described in chapter 4 for guidance.

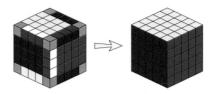

However, most people who have never attempted a 3×3×3 wouldn't dream of trying a 5×5×5, so I assume that you can already solve it. You will encounter no unusual cases or obstacles along the way; a normal 3×3×3 method is enough to finish off the Professor Cube. Well done!

TIPS FOR GETTING FASTER

Like the   4×4×4 method and the Revenge, the 5×5×5 method described above is a great method for solving your Professor Cube in the beginning. But if you want to solve it faster, you must become more efficient at the various steps.

Faster Centers

Speedcubers do not solve the centers of the 5×5×5 in the same way I describe above. While we do solve a center at a time, we are a lot more efficient in the way we do it. Most speedcubers tend to use the strategy of making 3×1 or 2×2 blocks and inserting them into the correct face. By placing several pieces together at a time, we can greatly reduce the number of moves needed to solve the centers. We use additional special tricks to solve the last 2 centers. The usual strategy is to first solve as many pieces as possible, and then know the shortest ways to solve the remaining center cubies. The fastest 5×5×5 solvers aim to solve the centers in about 30 to 35 seconds on average Table 8.12 demonstrates how a speedcuber would solve the first center of the Professor Cube.

Experiment on your own cube to investigate the strategy of solving many center pieces at once. With some experience, you will start to see various shortcuts of your own accord. The standard order to solve the centers is to solve the first center, then solve the opposite center, and

■ Table 8.12
5×5×5—Faster Centers Example

U-F-R View	D-B-L View

To solve the Yellow center, I first make a 3×1 block on the Yellow face. In doing so, I bring down the Yellow corner-center that is currently on the Yellow face.

Move: (L' l') U2 (L l)

Next I join up another 3×1 block in the middle layers by matching the corner-center on F with the 2×1 block of Yellow on R.

Move: F R (U' u')

Having formed the next 3×1 block, it is simply a matter of adding it to the Yellow face.

Move: U' (F' f')

All that remains is to join up the remaining 3 Yellow center cubies and insert them into the Yellow face.

Move: B' (U' u') B' D' (L l) B' (L l)

The first center is solved!

finally solve the remaining 4 centers in a ring around the middle. Because, unlike the 4×4×4, there is a fixed center piece, you immediately can recognize which colored center should go where.

Faster Tredges

By being clever about where you store solved tredges, taking special note of which unsolved edge pieces you are replacing, you can make the first-8-tredge method a bit more efficient. Rather than storing 4 in the U-layer, turning the cube upside down, and then storing 4 in the U-layer again, try to store the solved tredges in such a way that you bring down an edge piece of the same color as the next tredge you plan to solve. Table 8.13 shows an example.

By using this technique, we immediately reduce the number of moves, and therefore time, required to solve the tredges. It's all about moving fluently, looking ahead, and not pausing between storing 1 tredge and getting

■ **Table 8.13**
5×5×5—Faster Tredges Example

Yellow/Orange

In this example, I have just solved the Blue/Red tredge and am getting ready to store it in either the U-layer or D-layer. Since there is a random unsolved tredge in UF, I could just insert it into the U-layer as before (**R U′ R′**) and then begin the tredge-forming procedure all over again. However, I notice that the edge piece at uFL is Yellow/Orange, and I see the other Yellow/Orange wing edge at bUF. So if I insert the solved tredge using **F′ U F**, I have not only stored it safely but also brought the Yellow/Orange wing edge into the middle layers. It's then simply a matter of moving (**D′ d′**) to match up the 2 Yellow/Orange edges, finding the corresponding center edge, and then forming another tredge.

Move: **F′ U F**

ready to form the next. Try it out for yourself, slowly at first, until you get the hang of chaining the steps together.

Speedcubers also have some special tricks for solving the last 2 tredges. There are 10 cases in all, 6 without a parity error and 4 with. Table 8.14 gives the algorithms to solve these cases.

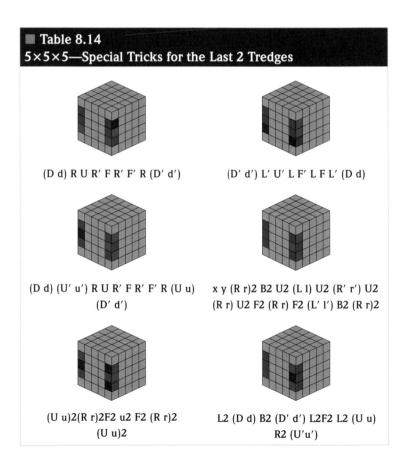

**■ Table 8.14
5×5×5—Special Tricks for the Last 2 Tredges**

(D d) R U R′ F R′ F′ R (D′ d′)

(D′ d′) L′ U′ L F′ L F L′ (D d)

(D d) (U′ u′) R U R′ F R′ F′ R (U u)
(D′ d′)

x y (R r)2 B2 U2 (L l) U2 (R′ r′) U2
(R r) U2 F2 (R r) F2 (L′ l′) B2 (R r)2

(U u)2(R r)2F2 u2 F2 (R r)2
(U u)2

L2 (D d) B2 (D′ d′) L2F2 L2 (U u)
R2 (U′u′)

x y (R r)2 B2 (R′ r′) U2 (R′ r′) U2 B2
(R′ r′) B2 (R r) B2 (R′ r′) B2 (R r)2

x y′ (L′ l′) U2 (L′ l′) U2 F2 (L′ l′)
F2 (R r) U2 (R′ r′) U2 (L l)2

x y (L l) U2 (L l)2 U2 (L′ l′) U2 (L
l) U2 (L′ l′) U2 (L l)2 U2 (L l)

x y (R′ r′) U2 (R r)2 U2 (R r) U2
(R′ r′) U2 (R r) U2 (R r)2 U2 (R′ r′)

To set up the various cases on your cube, just solve the tredges in your normal way and then invert the algorithms to get the corresponding case. Keep practicing, and you will soon get the hang of the faster tredge technique.

Faster 3×3×3 Phase

The advice for the 5×5×5 reduced 3×3×3 phase is very similar to that for the 4×4×4. The amount of time required to solve the 3×3×3 phase is mostly dependent on the method you use to solve a 3×3×3. If you use a beginner method, you will naturally need more time to complete the 3×3×3 phase than someone who uses the CFOP system with some advanced techniques. Because the 5×5×5 is a much larger cube than the 3×3×3, try to use more "wristy" turns, rather than finger tricks, which will tire out your fingers and increase the chance of pieces locking up and popping out. Other than that, there isn't really much to say apart from practice, practice, practice!

9 A Method to Solve Rubik's Mini Cube (2×2×2)

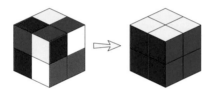

If you can already solve the 3×3×3, then you should have no problem with the 2×2×2. With a bit of thought, you can utilize some of the algorithms you know and apply them to the Mini Cube. Essentially, the 2×2×2 is the same as a 3×3×3 but without centers and edges, and the number of possible configurations is much smaller, coming in at only 3,674,160. Using expert methods, the fastest cubers in the world can solve this puzzle in 5 to 6 seconds on average. This chapter presents a simple method that allows even the most inexperienced puzzle solver to come to grips with this puzzle.

THINGS TO KNOW BEFORE YOU GET STARTED

If you haven't already done so, please familiarize yourself with the notation used to describe moves on the 2×2×2. This information can be found in chapter 3, "Cubing Notation."

The 2×2×2, like the 4×4×4, is an even cube and thus has no fixed centers. This means you decide what color the first face will be, and this determines the positions of the other colors. There is not much else to say, so let's get on with the solution.

THE GENERAL STRATEGY

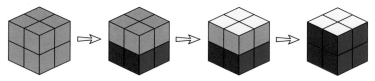

Solving the 2×2×2 is accomplished in 3 simple steps:

- **Solve 1 layer:** This is the same as solving the corners on the 3×3×3 and is achieved with 2 simple moves.
- **Solve the top face:** This step works in exactly the same way as twisting the top layer corners on the 3×3×3 and is again achieved very simply.
- **Solve the rest:** One further algorithm is required to solve the top layer, and hence the entire cube.

SOLVING THE BOTTOM LAYER

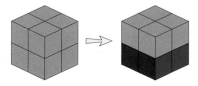

Choose a color to go on the bottom face, and then hold the cube so that there is at least 1 sticker of that color on the bottom face. Search the upper layer for other cubies with that color.

When you have found such a cubie, turn the U-layer so that it occupies the up-front-right (UFR) position, and then turn the D-layer to bring the position where it needs to go into the down-front-right position (DFR). You will then swap the piece in that position with the piece in the U-layer that has your bottom face color on it. See Table 9.1.

If there are no pieces with the bottom face color in the U-layer, turn the D-layer until an unsolved piece is at DFR. Then swap it with a random piece from the upper layer by using a trick from Table 9.1—the first algorithm is as good as any. When you have done this, you should have a piece in the upper layer that is the same color as the bottom face.

Repeat this procedure until the bottom layer is completely solved, and your cube should look something like Figure 9.1.

Make sure you have indeed solved the entire layer and not just the bottom face. If this isn't the case, then you have placed some pieces in the wrong destinations. Swap them back up into the upper layer using 1 of the tricks from the table, and then place them into the correct destination slots.

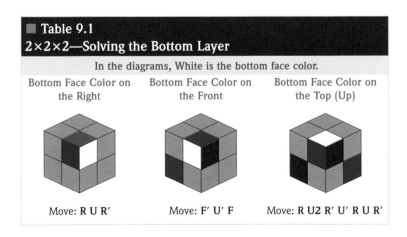

■ Table 9.1
2×2×2—Solving the Bottom Layer

In the diagrams, White is the bottom face color.

Bottom Face Color on the Right	Bottom Face Color on the Front	Bottom Face Color on the Top (Up)
Move: **R U R'**	Move: **F' U' F**	Move: **R U2 R' U' R U R'**

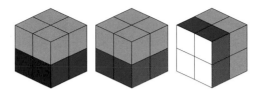

Figure 9.1 The solved bottom layer

SOLVING THE TOP FACE

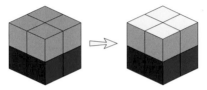

Make sure you know what color the top face is supposed to be before attempting this step. To identify the color, have a look at all the stickers on the upper layer—you will see 4 pairs of 2 colors and 1 set of 4 colors. The color of the "4-color" set is the top face color, which is obvious, if you think about it.

Hold the cube in your hands with the solved layer on the bottom, and whatever you do, don't rotate the cube in your hands while applying the next procedure! You will have to twist 2, 3, or 4 corners to solve the top face; it is impossible to have only 1 corner twisted. If no corners are twisted, the top face is already solved. In each case, you will twist the up-back-right (UBR) corners. See the diagrams in Table 9.2 for clarification.

This step is easy to get wrong. If you do make a mistake, it is likely that you will have to start from scratch. Apply the procedure carefully, and with a little bit of practice, you will soon be able to solve the top face with no problems. All that is left now is to position the top layer corners correctly.

■ Table 9.2
2×2×2—Solving the Top Face

The top face color in these diagrams is Yellow.

Top Face Color on the Right Side	Top Face Color on the Back

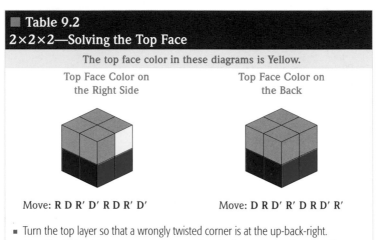

Move: **R D R′ D′ R D R′ D′**	Move: **D R D′ R′ D R D′ R′**

- Turn the top layer so that a wrongly twisted corner is at the up-back-right.
- Identify which of the 2 cases you have, and apply the corresponding algorithm.
- **Don't rotate the cube.** It will look like you have messed up your first layer, but don't worry. When you have finished solving the top face, your first layer will magically restore itself.
- Repeat this procedure to twist all the wrongly twisted corners in your top layer.

SOLVING THE TOP LAYER

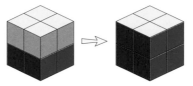

At this stage there are only 3 possible cases: 2 adjacent corners are swapped, 2 opposite corners are swapped, or the cube is solved. Identify which case you have from Table 9.3 and apply the corresponding algorithm to solve your cube.

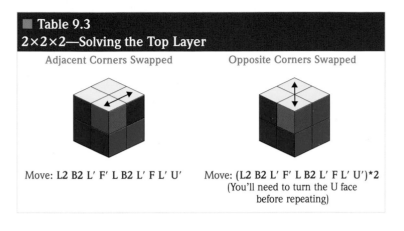

Table 9.3

2×2×2—Solving the Top Layer

Adjacent Corners Swapped	Opposite Corners Swapped
Move: **L2 B2 L′ F′ L B2 L′ F L′ U′**	Move: **(L2 B2 L′ F′ L B2 L′ F L′ U′)*2** (You'll need to turn the U face before repeating)

As you can see, there is just 1 algorithm to learn. In the case of the opposite corner swap, you just apply it 2 times.

If you made it this far, congratulations! Now there is nothing to stop you from being able to solve this puzzle faster and faster; all that is required is practice.

EXAMPLE SCRAMBLES AND SOLUTIONS

Start with a solved cube and apply the scramble algorithm with your chosen bottom face color on the bottom. Be sure to apply the scramble correctly, or the solution won't make much sense. Use the images in Table 9.4 as a guide only; if you scramble with Red on front and Yellow on up, then your cube should look like the diagram after scrambling. If you scramble with any other orientation, or you have a different color scheme, then it won't match the diagram exactly, but the pattern of colors should be the same.

■ Table 9.4
2×2×2—Example Solutions

Example Scramble 1: U' R2 F2 R' U2 F' U2 F' R' U R F2 U2 F R2

Solving the bottom layer:

- **D' U' F' U' F**
- **D R U R'**
- **D R U2 R' U' R U R'**

Solving the top face:

- **R D R' D' R D R' D'**
- **U' R D R' D' R D R' D'**
- **U' D R D' R' D R D' R'**
- **U' D R D' R' D R D' R'**

Solving the top layer:

- **y L2 B2 L' F' L B2 L' F L' U'**

Example Scramble 2: F' R U F U2 F' R F2 U2 F2 U' R' F' U' F

Solving the bottom layer:

- **z' U D F' U' F**
- **U2 D R U2 R' U' R U R'**
- **U2 D F' U' F**

Solving the top face:

- **U R D R' D' R D R' D'**
- **U D R D' R' D R D' R'**

Solving the top layer:

- **L2 B2 L' F' L B2 L' F L' U'**

10 General Tips

The last few chapters have concentrated heavily on the mechanics behind solving your cubes and solving them for speed. I would like to pass on a few more general tips, however, that you can apply not only to 1 particular puzzle but also to your speedsolving in general.

USE A "SPEED" CUBE

There is nothing more disheartening and frustrating than having to play with an old, rusty, worn-out cube, the sides of which are stiff and difficult to turn. Invest in a good, new cube. You could purchase a do-it-yourself kit from the Rubik's website and put together a good speedcube yourself, or you could buy one from a shop and hope that you are lucky enough to get a cube that turns nicely. Most, if not all, speedcubers treat their puzzle insides with silicon spray lubricant to make the sides spin even faster. You will also find that your cube becomes smoother the more you play with it as the rough edges inside gradually wear away. You can accelerate this process by sanding the insides of your cube very slightly, but don't overdo it, or you will make your cube too loose and unstable.

MEMORIZE ALGORITHMS WITH YOUR HANDS, NOT YOUR BRAIN

The sheer number of algorithms in the advanced system is daunting for the cubing novice. Each time you learn a new algorithm, make sure you are dead certain that you can recognize the case that the algorithm solves. Go through the algorithm several times, let your hands get used to the moves, and find an easy way to remember portions of the algorithm, such as a sequence of moves that you can execute in a single finger trick. Repeat the algorithm as much as possible—while watching TV, while waiting for a bus, even on the toilet if you are really keen. Eventually the algorithm will make the transition from your conscious memory to your subconscious muscle memory. Once you have achieved this, it is difficult to forget. You can memorize hundreds of algorithms this way, but it takes time and dedication.

The F2L algorithms are much more straightforward to learn than the OLL + PLL or more advanced algorithms, because it is easy to see what should be happening to the pieces with the F2L. If you understand the method behind the F2L algorithms, described in detail in chapter 6, then you should have no problem working out how to solve the F2L, even if you occasionally forget the algorithm itself. Over time, all the algorithms will seep into your muscle memory, until everything becomes automatic.

CUBING IS ABOUT A STATE OF MIND

In the beginning, you will have to give the cube 110% of your concentration and patience; it is hard work to recall the algorithms from memory when you are not used to them and haven't executed them hundreds of times. When you have practiced for a while, it will become much easier, and once you are used to solving the cube, it will feel more like a great way to kill time than agonizing, hard work. If you want to become a speedcuber and learn a speedcubing solution, you need a more professional approach. To cube fast and cube well, you must be relaxed enough so that you don't rush, because if you rush, you will make mistakes. However, don't relax too much, or you will lapse in concentration and also make mistakes. Always be positive, give each cube your full attention, and even if you do make a mistake never give up. It could be the rare occasion where the last layer is solved without you having to perform a single algorithm. This, by the way, has a probability of 1 in 15,552.

ACHIEVE THE RIGHT BALANCE BETWEEN SPEED AND FLUENCY

Speedcubers hit their best times when they achieve the perfect balance of speed and fluency. You obviously must turn quickly to solve the cube in a fast time, but the hands are quicker than the eyes, so it is quite possible to execute algorithms so rapidly that your eyes and brain can't keep up. When this happens, you will inevitably have to pause after each algorithm to look for the next pieces to solve, and introducing these delays impacts your overall solving time. If you slow down a bit, just enough so that your eyes and brain can keep up with what is happening to the cube, you will be able to determine the next pieces to solve while you are executing an algorithm ingrained in your muscle memory. By anticipating where the next pieces will be, and how they will be positioned on the cube, you can decide much more quickly which algorithm you should apply next. Using this technique, you can chain algorithms together to solve the whole of the cube, with next to no delays. The slower you turn, the easier this becomes, but of course, don't turn too slowly or you will impact your solving time. It's all about experimentation and finding the right balance.

CHECK INTERNET RESOURCES AND CHAT WITH OTHER CUBERS

Nowadays there are several great speedcubing resources on the Internet, written by dedicated speedcubers such as myself. I list some of my favorite websites at the end of this book, and from those sites you can find links to many more. Be sure to check them out; most of the best cubers have contact pages on their websites. You can get in touch with them and ask questions; speedcubers are always happy to help a fellow cuber.

Pretty Patterns

Y ou can make some very nice patterns with your cubes, and they make a great display piece on the coffee table. Start with a solved cube and use the algorithms in Table 11.1 to transform your cubes into a myriad of wonderful patterns.

Table 11.1
Pretty Pattern Algorithms

Pattern	Algorithm
	U2 D2 R2 L2 F2 B2

continued on next page

continued from previous page

Pattern	Algorithm
	(d D′ r R′)*4
	R2 L2 U D′ F2 B2 U D′
	R2 L2 U2 R2 L2 D2 F2 B2 U2 F2 B2 D2
	U2 R2 U2 D2 R2 U D
	U r′ R D2 F2 D2 r R′ U2 F2 U
	L′ F′ R′ L U D R′ D′ L′ B′ U2 L′ U′ R L U′ F2 R′

Pattern	Algorithm
	F L F U′ R U F2 L2 U′ L′ B D′ B′ L2 U
	U′ L′ U′ F′ R2 B′ R F U B2 U B′ L U′ F U R F
	L2 D2 L′ D2 B2 L2 B2 L′ D2 L2 B2 L′ B2
	L U B′ U′ R L′ B R′ F B′ D R D′ F′
	((r R′ U)*4 x y′)*3

This is by no means an exhaustive list of patterns; there are many thousands of pretty combinations you can make. Try them out, and see if you can make some different ones.

Glossary

' Notational suffix indicating that the preceding move token is in the counterclockwise direction

2-generator An algorithm that turns only 2 layers; the set of positions that can be reached by turning only 2 layers

2-look/3-look/4-look LL The number of distinct steps required to solve the last layer of a cube

algorithm A sequence of turns that always achieves a particular desired effect on the cube

average time In speedcubing, a cuber's average time is determined by solving the cube n times, n − 2 of which count. The fastest and the slowest times are removed, and the mean of the remaining times is calculated.

B-layer/face The back layer/face of the cube

big cubes The 4×4×4 and 5×5×5 cube puzzles

center piece The cubie that is at the direct center of a face, or in the case of the 4×4×4, the 4 cubies that surround the center point of a face

CFOP system Cross + First 2 Layers + OLL + PLL—an advanced system in speedcubing

COLL Corner Orient Last Layer—a set of algorithms that orients and permutes the corners of the last layer, without changing the orientation of the last layer edges

corner piece The cubies at the extreme corners of the puzzle. There are 8 of these on each cube, with 3 colors on each corner.

cross The first 4 edges solved in most layer-by-layer speedcubing solutions. When solved, they form a cross or plus shape on 1 of the faces.

cubie The individual pieces that make up the whole cube puzzle

cycle The act of changing the positions of pieces—for example, in the original piece configuration A-B-C, those pieces are shuffled to occupy the positions C-A-B, or B-C-A

D-layer/face The bottom layer/face of the cube. D stands for "down."

E-layer The middle layer of the cube between the U- and D-layers; thought to stand for "equator"

edge piece An individual piece of a cube puzzle that has 2 colors. There are $12 (n - 2)$ edges on an $n \times n \times n$ cube.

F-layer/face The front layer/face of the cube

face A 2-dimensional side of the cube, made up of 1 unique color when the puzzle is solved

finger trick A combination of moves that can be executed very rapidly since they can be triggered in the same hand movement

First 2 Layers/F2L The D-layer and E-layer of the cube; the term to describe the solving of the D-layer and E-layer simultaneously

flip To physically change the orientation of an edge, or the actual orientation state of the edge

Fridrich method/system A commonly used alternative name for the CFOP system

inverse An algorithm written or executed in reverse

last layer/LL The final layer to solve in any layer-by-layer system— usually the U-layer

layer A 3-dimensional slice of the cube, made up of all the cubies that move when a portion of the puzzle is turned

layer-by-layer An approach to solving the cube that involves solving a layer at a time

L-layer/face The left layer/face of the cube

lucky case A speedsolve in which 1 or more parts are skipped due to luck

move A turn of 1 of the layers of the cube

orientation (*see* flip *and* twist) The physical act of twisting a piece without necessarily affecting its position; the current state of the piece's orientation relative to the rest of the puzzle

Orient(ation) Last Layer/OLL The stage in the CFOP system where the orientations of the last layer pieces are corrected

orientation parity (fix) A case on the big cubes where the edge orientation appears to violate the rules of parity, when considering the $3 \times 3 \times 3$ reference frame; the algorithm to fix such a case

parity Relationship between the orientations and permutations of edges and corners

permutation The physical act of changing the position of a piece, without necessarily affecting its orientation

Permute Last Layer/PLL The stage in the CFOP system where the positions of all the last layer pieces are corrected

permutation parity (fix) A case on the big cubes where the edge permutation appears to violate the rules of parity, when considering the $3\times3\times3$ reference frame; the algorithm to fix such a case

Pocket Cube The $2\times2\times2$ version of Rubik's Cube

Professor Cube The $5\times5\times5$ version of Rubik's Cube

R-layer/face The right layer/face of the cube

Revenge Cube The $4\times4\times4$ version of Rubik's Cube

rotation The physical act of turning the whole cube, without turning the individual layers

Rubik's Cube The original $3\times3\times3$ cubical puzzle

side *See* face

speedcuber A person who solves Rubik's Cube and related twisty puzzles against the clock

speedcubing/speedsolving The art of solving Rubik's Cube and related twisty puzzles as fast as possible

trigger Another name for a finger trick

twist To physically change the orientation of a corner, or the actual orientation state of the corner

U-layer/face The up(per) layer/face of the cube

VH system An advanced system for solving Rubik's Cube invented by Lars Vandenbergh and Dan Harris

World Cube Association (WCA) The governing body of all official speedcubing competitions

x A cube rotation in the direction of R

y A cube rotation in the direction of U

z A cube rotation in the direction of F

ZB system An advanced system for solving Rubik's Cube invented independently by Zbigniew Zborowski and Ron van Bruchem

Further Resources

SPEEDCUBING WEBSITES

http://www.cubestation.co.uk The author's website.

http://www.speedcubing.com Website by WCA co-founder Ron van Bruchem from The Netherlands; probably the biggest single resource for speedcubing on the Internet.

http://www.solvethecube.co.uk Website by 2006 European champion and multiple tournament winner Joël van Noort from The Netherlands; contains a lot of useful algorithms and tools.

http://www.cubezone.be Website by 2004 European champion and Square-1 world record holder Lars Vandenbergh from Belgium; lots of useful information, including his Square-1 system.

http://www.geocities.com/jaapsch/puzzles Website by puzzle enthusiast Jaap Scherphuis of The Netherlands; has information on an extensive range of puzzles, including solutions.

http://www.thepublicvoid.com 2003 world champion Dan Knights' website.

http://www.stefan-pochmann.info/spocc/ Great website by Germany's Stefan Pochmann, who has held multiple world records over the years.

http://www.ws.binghamton.edu/fridrich/cube.html Website by Jessica Fridrich, developer of the Fridrich method and 1982/2003 World Championship finalist.

http://www.lar5.com/cube The Petrus method, by 1982 World Championship finalist Lars Petrus.

http://grrroux.free.fr/method/Intro.html The Roux method, by Gilles Roux.

http://www.geocities.com/jasmine_ellen/RubiksCube Solution.html A great beginner solution by Australian champion Jasmine Lee.

http://www.worldcubeassociation.org Website of the official governing body of speedcubing; contains a fantastic database of all official competitions and competition results.

SPEEDCUBING FORUMS
http://games.groups.yahoo.com/group/speedsolving rubikscube/ The most established international speedcubing Internet forum.

http://www.speedsolving.com/ Another fantastic forum and resource for speedcubing.

http://twistypuzzles.com/forum/ A more general forum, for both speedcubers and puzzle enthusiasts/collectors.

WHERE TO BUY PUZZLES AND PUZZLE ACCESSORIES
http://www.rubiks.com The official site of the Rubik's brand.

http://www.cubesmith.com A puzzle accessory website with top-quality products from Chris Licciardi; a great place to buy new stickers when yours wear out!

Index